# *The* SIGN *of the* BUFFALO SKULL

## The Story of Jim Bridger, Frontier Scout

### By PETER O. LAMB

*With fourteen illustrations in black-and-white by*
JAMES DAUGHERTY

FREDERICK A. STOKES COMPANY

NEW YORK                    MCMXXXII

STEALING HORSES

# CONTENTS

# CONTENTS

## PART IV. CHIEF SCOUT

# FOREWORD

THE tradition of American scouting is founded in the exploits of Boone, Carson and Bridger. To millions of Boy Scouts they have been the supreme heroes, illustrating in their adventures the sturdiness of the scout qualities, and the wisdom of scoutcraft.

Boone and Carson dictated short accounts of their adventures. From Jim Bridger not a single word has come down to us. A gun, a buffalo robe, a short business letter signed with his mark, are about the only personal mementoes of Bridger that remain with us.

In his day Bridger was a fable in the mountains and on the plains. Those who knew him best felt that his adventures were so numerous, his skill as an Indian fighter, scout and guide so great that no frontiersmen who ever lived could compare with him, not Carson, not even Boone.

Such comparisons are not for us. Each played his part as he found it supremely well, and Bridger in his lifetime would have been the first to decry any effort to extol him at the expense of another. It is very likely that Daniel

Boone was one of Bridger's boyhood heroes, for Boone was a celebrated figure in the Missouri days when Jim was working around the farm, and serving out his apprenticeship to a blacksmith in St. Louis. He knew Boone's son, and probably a number of Boone's grandsons who adventured in the mountains that were Jim Bridger's home.

As to Carson—that sandy-haired youngster and Jim Bridger had celebrated Kit's joining Bridger's trappers by a chase of some horse-stealing Blackfoot. Kit had a wound—his only one—to show for that experience. Bridger had contributed something to Kit's trail education in the subsequent hunts, and must have taken great pride when Kit told him, during a little excursion they made together in 1850, of his California experiences with Fremont. How Bridger must have chuckled when Kit spoke of his embarrassment at finding himself a social lion in Washington when he was sent to the capital with dispatches for President Polk!

The stories of each of these frontiersmen come down to us in scattered fragments. A large part of Bridger's adventures are completely lost; we can only infer their extent. To estimate his Indian fights is to arrive at an unbelievable total. Since much of this happened during long years in an isolated mountain region, a thousand miles from the nearest settlements, it is impossible to-day to reconstruct more than a fraction of them.

Certain it is that during strenuous years spent in the Rockies Bridger garnered an incomparable knowledge of the Indian; of the redman's methods of warfare and how best to combat them; skill and craft as guide and scout that was unequaled in his day; and a peerless knowledge of the topography of a vast country which he traversed as a trapper and explorer.

In presenting this modest narrative regarding Jim Bridger,—for many years there has been a call from boy readers for a story of the great scout,—the author wishes to express his obligation to the many sources from which he has drawn his material, and especially to Dr. Grace Raymond Hebard and Mr. J. Cecil Alter, who have done so much to bring to light information regarding the man who in his day was persistently referred to, among western frontiersmen, as "the most distinguished of them all."

# PART I

## TENDERFOOT

# THE SIGN OF THE BUFFALO SKULL

## CHAPTER I

### THE NEW FRONTIER

JIM BRIDGER was born in Richmond, Va., on March 17, 1804, the youngest of a family of three children, two boys and a girl. He was named after his father, James, who with his wife, Chloe, and the little family lived on a farm in the outskirts of the Virginia capital. They were people of some substance, for in addition to the farm they owned an inn. Mrs. Bridger was related in some way to President Tyler.

James Bridger, the elder, was by profession a surveyor. The pioneering instinct ran strong in him, and like so many of the sturdy men of that day, his eyes turned westward. Not Kentucky now, nor Ohio and Indiana and Illinois. These were part of the new republic. The adventurous young men of the east were looking beyond those boundaries to Missouri.

The year before Jim was born, Napoleon Bonaparte, then First Consul of France, but with a wary eye on the title of Emperor, had sold to the United States for fifteen million dollars the entire territory of Louisiana, a vast area of land, over one million square miles, and stretching from the Gulf of Mexico to the Canadian border. The year the great scout was born, President Jefferson persuaded Congress to appropriate two thousand five hundred dollars to send an expedition that would pass through this territory overland to the Pacific, and chose for the task two men for whose capabilities he had high regard. Lewis and Clark made an epic journey up the Missouri River, returning by the same route inside of two years. Zebulon M. Pike, after whom the great peak in the Rockies is named, made his westward journey the year they returned. Reports of the great number of fur-bearing animals in the new coun-

try brought the adventurous traders Manuel
Lisa and John Jacob Astor into the picture.
Thus began one of the most romantic chapters
in our conquest of the west.

Young Jim's recollections of the first conver-
sations he heard by the family fireside must have
been of the ways and means of settling up their
affairs and making the journey to the far frontier settlement of Missouri. There had been
much talk of roads to be built towards the west.
Money for the purpose had even been set aside
by Congress, but nothing was done, or would be
done, for several years. The farm and inn had
to be sold; much of the furniture, too, for transportation by land was slow and cumbersome;
the cost prohibitive.

There were regular stage lines between the
big towns and since it was the easiest way to
make the journey it is likely that the Bridgers
traveled in that way from Richmond to Washington, then on to Baltimore, Philadelphia and
Pittsburgh. These cities, even then giving evidence of the lines along which they were to
develop, seem to have made little impression on
the eight-year-old Jim. He never longed for
them; he seldom even spoke of them in later
years.

The new world that had captured James

Bridger's enthusiasm, began at Pittsburgh. On Jim it was to write its impression so deep that the instinct for the wilderness became a second nature to him.

From Pitts-town, even then the smoky city, the keelboats ran down the Ohio River. The year previous a Mr. Roosevelt built a steamboat after the pattern of those running on the Hudson River and it had made a triumphal journey all the way to New Orleans, but it was a few years yet before a regular steamboat service was to be established. In 1812 when the Bridgers made their journey the keelboat was the normal craft to Cincinnati or some near-by point, where the passengers changed into flatboats that ran the falls at Louisville. The flatboats were continued for the rest of the journey, down the Ohio and the Mississippi, being usually broken up at New Orleans.

The journey down the Ohio was young Bridger's first taste of the wilderness. Through much of it Kentucky lay on the left bank, as they crept slowly past the plains of Ohio, Illinois and Indiana. There were many settlements, of course, and numerous isolated farms from which a settler would sometimes hail the boat offering to barter some of his produce for the things manufactured in the cities. There were long stretches, however, that were still the wilderness—treeless plains rolling to the horizon, miles of dense woods. Everywhere there was evidence of the plentitude of game, and possibly a deer or two contributed to the fresh meat supply of the passengers. Though the tiny youngster could remember in after years almost nothing of that journey, we may be sure that for son as well as father it had the warming quality of the new adventure they had set out to find.

Up the Mississippi, from the point where the Ohio flows into the "father of waters" to St. Louis, an old French settlement, the Bridger family journeyed. St. Louis was only a small place then. Its two thousand inhabitants were largely dependent at that time, as they were to be enriched later, on the fur trade.

The Bridgers had chosen an inauspicious time to migrate. War against England was declared by the United States. There was a great deal of concern in those far outposts. They were at the mercy of an Indian uprising if it were made in force, and it was feared that the British would instigate, if they did not lead, the Indians to attack the frontier settlements. These fears proved groundless. People like Manuel Lisa, who in addition to his fur trading was an Indian agent, were able to keep the redmen friendly.

The few warlike demonstrations made by the Indians did not prove of any importance. The vigorous development that had been in progression during the thirty years in which the new United States had been a nation, however, came to a standstill. There was little call for the elder Bridger's services as a surveyor. They lived for a while at St. Louis, then moved to a farm at Six-Mile Prairie. Land in that day could be bought for a dollar or two an acre.

The treaty which terminated the war was signed at Ghent in 1814. News in that day traveled very slowly, and hostilities continued for many months longer. Much of what had happened during the war had been too far away to stir the people on this far frontier. Their chance did not come until the year following the formal treaty of peace, when General Andrew Jackson fought the battle of New Orleans. Old Hickory's backwoods riflemen, standing behind their breastworks, and firing with deadly accuracy, tore great gaps in the advancing British ranks. The Americans were outnumbered nearly three to one. They had 3,918 men to the British 10,084. The losses were even more disproportionate. The British lost in killed and wounded, 3,336 including three generals, to the loss of but 21 men killed and wounded among

Old Hickory's men. The battle had many elements of romance, but to the frontier it was home-town stuff, the striking prowess of its own borderers. St. Louis and near-by settlements rang their bells, had special services, illuminated their houses and streets. Young Jim Bridger felt that this was the greatest battle that had ever been fought. Later as a boy he must have met a number of the men who served with Jackson, and learned many of the details of that famous battle. They made a deep impression on his mind.

With the end of the war business began to hum again. Astoria, where John Jacob Astor had established a trading post in 1811, during the war had struck its flag to the British, but Lisa and other traders had carried on, as did a few men who were free-trappers. There were many calls now for the elder James Bridger as a surveyor and he had to be constantly on the move. Consequently much of the man's work on the farm had to be done by Jim and his brother.

Jim Bridger never went to school, and to the end of his days he could neither read nor write, although it is possible that he was able to letter his name for he once carved it on a rock. Very few people in our frontier settlements had these accomplishments. It was only the accident of an ambitious sister-in-law that had led to Daniel Boone learning to read and write. Kit Carson was about fifty years old when he learned his letters. Not only was the frontier handicapped by the want of schools, but there was a spirit among the backwoodsmen similar to the attitude with which the knights and lords of feudal times regarded the arts of reading and writing. They had little need for them in their occupations. When such knowledge was necessary they could hire people for a trifling sum to do what was necessary. The possession of these arts could not win fame or fortune for the backwoodsman any more than they could win them for the knights, and his concern and ambition turned in the direction of acquiring the knowledge and arts that would serve him best in his daily life, or help him to accomplish the things he was ambitious to do. A mind as active and quick as Jim Bridger's could have learned the rudiments of reading and writing in short order had he felt any incentive to do so at any time during his life.

This early experience on the farm gave Bridger some knowledge of agriculture, and developed an interest that he never quite lost. To-day we would probably consider the life a boy led in that day a pretty hard routine for a youngster, but it all contributed to building a strong, supple body, groundwork for the phenomenal powers of endurance he was later to display.

It was here on the farm that he laid the foundations of two things that helped to make him the most celebrated of our mountain men. He learned to shoot, becoming a good shot even as a boy; and he unconsciously developed keen faculties of observation. Because of the frequent absences of his father, upon him and his brother must have fallen the task of hunting for the larder; possibly, too, there was some trapping on the river. It was the horse country, and riding and caring for them was an everyday necessity.

Observation as our frontiersmen, and especially scouts, practised it is to-day a lost art. It was a complicated business of making every bird and animal and tree tell you the story of what had happened recently or what was happening at the moment. Not your eyes alone must be quick to note a thousand details, but your ears must be alert to distinguish among a thousand sounds, your nose to emulate the sensitiveness of a deer, your foot to feel the earth with the clutching softness of a panther, your hands to recognize a hundred things by touch alone.

In Jim Bridger's day as a boy the frontier had

a unique tradition of marksmanship, and we must read the statement that he was even then a good shot in the light of that tradition. The modern high velocity bullet, the repeating rifle, and the passing of the necessity of hunting as the only means of supplying ourselves with meat, have brought great changes in our standards of marksmanship. A junior marksman to-day qualifies with putting twenty shots into the inner circle of the standard target—or its equivalent —with a .22 rifle, at fifty feet, ten shots fired standing, ten lying flat on the ground. This is good shooting, but it differs greatly from frontier standards.

In Bridger's early Missouri the tradition of the Kentucky rifle and its riflemen ran strong. A great many of the pioneers here had crossed over from that state. The long rifle was still used, the only difference in the gun was that the flint lock was being changed to take the new percussion cap.

Loading was then an essential part of rifle skill. The expert could go through the whole business, aim and fire his weapon in thirty seconds. There were a dozen motions he had to make: blow down the barrel to make sure the nipple was clear; pour the powder in from the horn, ram it down, set his patch and ball and ram that down, look to the priming, set the cap, aim and fire. Every movement had to be carried out with a careful and steady hand. If the priming was not just right the result would be a hang-fire, that is, there would be a momentary delay between the explosion of the cap and the powder charge. If the powder was poor and the priming very bad the cap would fail altogether to explode the powder. Anyone who has fired an old muzzle-loader knows how easy it is for this to happen; yet these "accidents" were almost unheard of among the border riflemen who loaded their rifles even while running and riding. Our frontiersmen had to be accurate when they shot. They lacked the advantage we have to-day of being able to throw another cartridge in the breech of a repeater with a jerk of the hand. The point blank range was about a hundred yards, whereas to-day our rifles are easily good for two or three times that distance without an adjustment of the sights. Beyond that range they had to allow for the drop of the bullet. There was a premium, therefore, on the study of distance, windage, on the quality of the powder used, on the size of the load and the bullet; above all on careful, accurate shooting, and the tradition of these riflemen carried it to a superlative excellence.

We have already seen something of its deadly effect at the battle of New Orleans. Small game, a bird or a squirrel, would only be shot through the head. The latter was sometimes barked, that is, the bullet was aimed at the bark under the squirrel, the concussion somersaulting it in the air and bringing it down dead. The great sport of that day was the rifle-shooting match. At forty paces, one out of three shots of these expert riflemen, would drive a nail in at the head, and another touch it. They fired at targets and had many other standard tests. There was a practical turn to such shooting matches, too. Snuffing a candle was a night test. A writer who observed such a match states that at fifty yards, three out of seven shots put out the candle, remarkable shooting with no daylight view of their sights. The value of this was in night shooting, what was called "flashing." An animal whose eyes flashed against the light of a campfire would be hit between the eyes. Such a shot once cost Jim Bridger, the tenderfoot, a year's salary. He fired at the flash of a pair of eyes and found that he had killed a valuable mule.

Everything around young Jim Bridger was calling him to an adventure in the mountains. The chanting voyageurs who passed up and down the river bordering the farm; the devil-may-care, swaggering free-trapper; the traders growing wealthy with the harvest of beaver skins; the tradition of the trail-breakers. Old Daniel Boone, long a fable of the frontier, was living near by, and you may be sure Bridger knew about him, for Missouri was immensely proud of Boone's residence in the territory. When a few years later Boone died, the first legislature of the State of Missouri was in session at St. Louis. It adjourned out of respect to his memory, representatives and senators going into mourning. Bridger was then sixteen and resident at St. Louis. Long before then, however, the desire to set out west had moved him to action.

At twelve he took matters into his own hand and attached himself to a trapping party. The whole incident comes down to us in a confused way, as do a great many of the facts we know about Jim Bridger. He told of the incident when he was about sixty years old to men who set it down thirty or forty years later, so that it is mixed up with later happenings. The trappers in the party were, of course, unwilling to take a youngster with them on so arduous a journey. Bridger let them make a start, then taking a blanket and some jerky—the dried venison that was a staple of trail-fare—he followed on foot, making his own camp near by at night. He repeated this the following day and the next, and walked into the camp when they were a hundred miles out. Some of the men were of the opinion that since the boy had made his way alone he should be asked to make his way back the same way, but the leader decided that since he had shown so much pluck he should be taken along. If this is correct, Bridger would not have returned until the following year, just in time for a series of family tragedies that was to alter the course of his young ambition.

His mother died and soon after that his brother. A few months later his father died. At thirteen Jim Bridger became the man of the family, feeling keenly his responsibility to his sister and the aunt who had come out to look after them. He tried running a flatboat ferry from the farm at Six-Mile Prairie to St. Louis. It was too much for so young a boy, and he was forced to give it up, and to apprentice himself to a blacksmith named Phil Creamer. Whatever his dreams of adventure on plains and mountains had been he put them aside, and faithfully carried out the contract made for him. He served Creamer five years. It was a trade that was to be of some use to him in later years, as was his experience on the farm. The pioneering instinct still ran strong in him, although dormant in these apprentice years. When the time came he was able to step out from it into an adventure probably much bigger than any he had dreamed about in the strenuous days on the farm and at the forge.

## CHAPTER II

### BLACKFEET BAR THE WAY

WE know very little regarding Phil Creamer or of Bridger's life during his apprenticeship to him. They gave each other a friendly and faithful service. The artisan of that day not only taught his apprentices his trade, making them, of course, pay their way with work, but he made himself responsible for their social, recreational, and often religious activities. The boys sometimes lived in the master's own household, and when this was not possible he arranged for their board and lodging for which he paid, and kept an eye on their comings and goings. Hours of work

were long, but there must have been enough opportunity for recreation and sport, for during
this period Bridger kept developing those frontiersmen's arts to which we have already made
passing reference.

The blacksmith shop of that day was a great
deal more than a horse-shoeing establishment.
Nails were made here, all the iron work re-
quired for houses, ploughs, and a great many
other things, including beaver and other traps
which were an all important commodity in St.
Louis. Young Bridger while at the shop must
have become acquainted with a great many of
the free-trappers and river men who adventured
up the Missouri (these hard-bitten adven-
turers sometimes made the town very lively with
their presence); some of Old Hickory's backwoodsmen, too; and it is possible even that he
here became acquainted with some of the men
with whom his fortune was to be cast: General
William Ashley, Major Andrew Henry, the Sublette boys, Bill the elder five years Bridger's
senior and Milt nearer his own age, Provot,
Hugh Glass, even Mike Fink, and those three
musketeers whose names appear on every daring
expedition—Rezner, Hoback and Robinson.
They had trapped with Henry in the early days,
joined the Astor Overlanders in the trek across

the mountains and back, and were ready for any other adventurous call that was to be made.

In any case the blacksmith's shop would be one of the first places to hear of a new and ambitious venture that was taking shape. Manuel Lisa, with his Missouri Fur Company, was the big name in the trapping business at St. Louis. Lisa was Indian agent too; he traded for furs with them, giving cheap beads and mirrors, which the Indians valued highly, some powder and shot, in exchange for valuable beaver and other skins, which they valued not at all. He also took trapping parties, consisting mainly of French voyageur-hunters, who worked out from his stations on the Missouri and Yellowstone. Lisa had tried including American trappers on some of his expeditions. Andrew Henry had been once his partner, but the impression one gathers from one trapper who made a record of his adventures, is that the Americans disliked Lisa and were plainly contemptuous of the Frenchmen he employed, the voyageurs who lived on bacon instead of he-man buffalo meat, and who were so timid that they trapped only within hailing distance of the "forts"!

Yet, the resourceful and bold free-trapper almost inevitably turned out a victim of his own

intrepidity. There is an estimate that three out
of four of these men lost their lives, to Indians
principally. John Colter, a man of remarkable
adventures, who left the Lewis and Clark expedition and plunged into the unknown Rockies
on a lonely trapping expedition, had been driven
out by the Blackfeet, and glad he was to escape
with his life. Andrew Henry, who was now
running the lead mines General Ashley was interested in, had had a similar experience when
as Lisa's partner he had taken a party to the
headwaters of the Yellowstone.

Everybody knew there was a gold mine of
beaver in the mountains—a pelt was bringing
from six to eight dollars then in St. Louis—but
neither Lisa's plan nor the free-trapper in small
parties had proved themselves adequate. A
party large enough to maintain itself and trans-
port its catch was necessary. They had to be
men of spirit for the natural dangers of the
mountain country, and the menace of roving
bands of Indians was so great that every attempt
so far to leave the main streams had ended in
near-disaster. Consequently there must have
been a great deal of excited talk in St. Louis in
the winter of 1821-22 as word of the plans that
General William H. Ashley and Andrew Henry
were making got about. Since the expedition

they planned must have included in its equipment thousands of new traps, it is possible that even then Phil Creamer's shop was making some of them. Ashley and Henry were men well in the forties, mature men, respected in the community in which they had been long resident, Ashley coming originally from Virginia and Henry from his native state of Pennsylvania. They were both officers in the local militia. General Ashley was one of the prominent business men of the town, a banker, and could command all the capital the venture would require. Henry having had practical knowledge of the country became the ideal leader to take charge of such a venture while in the field.

Their celebrated advertisement

> To enterprising young men. The subscriber wishes to engage one hundred young men to ascend the Missouri River to its source, there to be employed for one, two or three years. For particulars inquire of Major Andrew Henry, near the lead mines in the county of Washington, who will ascend with and command the party; or of the subscriber near St. Louis. Signed—William H. Ashley.

appeared in the Missouri Republican of March 20th, 1822, but it was probably only the final winding up of their plans, for within twenty-five days the expedition had set out, a land and water party, with Jim Bridger the youngest of that motley crowd that was to make history.

This was not a Jim Bridger straining at the leash towards adventure, but a youngster sobered by years of discipline and a sense of responsibility. The thought that was uppermost in his mind was that now at last he could support his sister. The pay of these "enterprising men" was not very great even for that time; by our standards it seems unbelievably meager. Seasoned veterans could be hired for four hundred dollars a year; less experienced men received no more than two hundred dollars for a whole twelve months' service, so that Jim had not by any means stepped into a fortune. He was eighteen years old. His figure had probably not yet set; but under the gawkiness of the maturing boy one could see the man. He was nearly six feet in height, straight as an Indian, strong and slender, weighing about one hundred and fifty or sixty pounds. His gray eyes had a tinge of blue in them in certain lights. He had a mop of brown hair that a thousand braves, Blackfoot and Sioux and fighting Cheyennes were to look at enviously as a trophy for their scalp belt.

Spare horses and mounted trappers formed

the land party.  Supplies were carried in two
keelboats, slender vessels about seventy-five feet
long and about fifteen broad, drawing two or
three feet of water, and decked over except for
a space at bow and stern.  The journey upstream on the winding Missouri was a slow business, a voyage not without its dangers, but long
a traveled highway.  There was even a little
christening ceremony in vogue among the rivermen similar to the practice of sailors on crossing the equator, which each new voyageur had
to undergo the first time he went north of the
point where the Platte River flows into the Missouri.

The keelboats used sails wherever possible
strange as that may seem in river navigation.  In
a calm, if in deep water and near the shore, the
*cordelle* was used to tow the vessel.  Cordelle
was the voyageur's name for a rope running
from the bow to the mast, and from there passed
on shore high above the bushes.  A string of men
walking on the shore hauled the boat along.
When the keelboat was becalmed in the middle
of the stream in deep water, oars were resorted
to, two lines of rowers set well forward of mid-
ships keeping the boat moving.

In shallow water, when it was impossible to
sail, the keelboats were punted.  The men stood

at the bow on a narrow walk along both gun-
wales.  At a signal the long poles would be
thrust into the sand or mud.  The top end of
the pole, rounded and smooth, was caught by
each man in the hollow of his outer shoulder,
and all pushed steadily towards the stern.  At a
signal poles would be hauled out simultaneously,
all walk back to the bow, and start over again.
The steersman sitting on a high seat in the stern
called the necessary orders and bossed the crew.

These rivermen, voyageurs, were chiefly
Frenchmen, a little timid by trapper standards,
but gay and adventurous; a singing crowd.  All
their movements were carried out to a rollicking
chant, meaningless nonsense most of it, but not
without its charm.  The verses were endless, the
leader, one best able to extemporize.  Here are
two verses of one of these French chants:

> LEADER:  On my way I encountered
> Three cavaliers gaily mounted.
> Chorus:  Lon, ton, laridon, danée.
> Lon, ton, laridon, dai.
> Three cavaliers, gaily mounted.
> One on a horse, one on foot!

The dangers on the river were chiefly from
shoals, from great logs sticking out from the
shore or imbedded in the mud of the streams.

Skillful navigation was necessary. That this danger was very real, the expedition was soon to learn, for in mid-stream one of the boats struck a submerged log and sank, the entire cargo, worth about ten thousand dollars, being completely lost.

That was the first trouble the expedition was to encounter. The second was equally serious. At a place that is near what is now Bismarck, North Dakota, the Assiniboine Indians, made friendly advances, then stole fifty of the expedition's horses. The expedition went on, however to the confluence of the Yellowstone, near what is now the Montana border. There on a tongue of land, Henry started to build a fort, while Ashley, who had accompanied the expedition, returned to St. Louis, intending to return the next year with supplies and another complement of men.

Not all the fall was given to the building of the fort, of course. The men on the expedition were a mixed assortment of hard, seasoned veterans and tenderfeet; many young men of good family and education having been drawn to the enterprise as well as some "tough hombres." Before the streams froze over towards the end of December there was some trapping and hunting, setting plans for defence against Indian raids, seasoning generally for the tough work ahead of them in the spring. There was a little trading with friendly Indians. The winter and early spring at Fort Henry, as it was called, comes down to us without the chronicle of any striking experiences, except for the remarkable story of Mike Fink, Carpenter and Talbot, who had taken service with the expedition to serve as both rivermen and trappers.

These three men were desperate characters, remarkable shots. Fink in particular had a reputation that marked him out even among the hard-boiled. He took every opportunity to get drunk, and "likkered" he was a terror. Many tales were told of his desperate fights. He had an uncomfortable sense of humor. Seeing a negro on the streets of St. Louis with a protrusion of flesh on his heel, Fink cut it cleanly with a ball from his rifle, and pleaded to the magistrate before whom he was haled that he did so in order that the darkey might be able to wear a "genteel" boot. When his wife displeased him, he collected a great pile of leaves, forced her at the point of his gun to lie in the middle of them, then set fire to the pile in several places. When the flames finally forced her to brave his gun, her clothes were afire, and as she plunged into the river he shouted after her: "There, that will teach you not to make eyes at the other rivermen."

When they were drunk Fink and his pal Carpenter took a unique way of showing their affection for each other. At a measured seventy paces, a mug of whisky, with a black spot marked slightly above the water line, would be set on the head of one, while the other plugged a hole in the tin with a rifle ball, the perfect accomplishment being a bullet through the black mark, and a head held so steady that not a drop of whisky was lost!

These men chose to make their camp outside Fort Henry during the winter, and there Fink and Carpenter fell into a bitter quarrel. When the first thaw brought them into the fort, they managed to get hold of some whisky, and warmed by it Fink suggested the usual mark of their affection. This time, however, Carpenter was certain that Mike intended treachery. Carpenter told Talbot this, and willed Talbot his gun and pistols. Sure as Carpenter was that Fink intended foul play, his code would not allow him to withdraw from the test, and he went into it without any nervousness.

A copper was tossed up in the air and the first shot fell to Fink. Calling out to Carpenter to "hold his noodle steady" and to be sure not to

drop any of that whisky because he wanted to
drink it, Fink aimed and fired, the ball striking Carpenter in the center of the forehead and
killing him instantly.   As Carpenter fell, Mike
Fink is reported to have called out, "you have
spilt the whisky," and calmly blew down his
gun to clear the nipple and the barrel of smoke.
When told that Carpenter was dead, he began
to curse, and to swear that he took as true an
aim on the black center as he had ever done on
a squirrel's eye.

Talbot thrust Carpenter's pistol into his belt,
and said never a word.   Some time later, Mike
in his cups, boasted in Talbot's presence that he
had deliberately shot Carpenter, and Talbot
drawing Carpenter's pistol from his belt, shot
the Irishman dead.   Talbot himself was drowned
while swimming a river some months later,
while still with the Ashley-Henry Expedition.

The expedition had come out to trap the headwaters of the Missouri.   As soon as spring began
to thaw the river, Henry took his men upstream
to harvest the prime spring furs.   At Great Falls
he came up against his old enemies, the Blackfeet.   One of his company leaders was killed as
were three or four others in the fight that ensued.   The Blackfeet outnumbered his force, so
Henry retired on his fort, turning his back on

the rich beaver streams to wait Ashley's reënforcements and supplies.

What he received instead, was a hurry call for
help. Young Jedediah Smith, fresh from the
east, and a veteran trapper, came riding post-
haste with news that the Arikara ('Rees) Indians had fallen on a detachment of forty trappers belonging to Ashley's party which was
accompanying the boats, that the Indians had
killed half the number, and looted them of most
of their property, including the horses. Ashley
had tried to rally his voyageurs to attack the Indians, but they had no stomach for a fight, and
it was all he could do to hold them some little
distance downstream, while Smith rode to
Major Henry, and another messenger reported
the outrage to Col. Henry Leavenworth at the
nearest military post.

Henry, with eighty men, among them young
Jim Bridger, started down country immediately.
It happened that Col. Leavenworth, commanding the troops of the region, was getting ready to
discipline this very tribe of Indians because of
similar outrages, so he was able to act immediately. When he came upstream with 250 troopers, bringing three cannon by boat, he was joined
by sixty men belonging to Lisa's Missouri Fur
Company, and a large body of friendly Sioux

SCALP DANCE

eager to take part in a battle against an enemy tribe.

Ashley's men now numbered about two hundred, and it looked as if the 'Rees were going to be taught a sanguinary lesson. But plans went all awry. The Sioux formed the center of Leavenworth's line of attack. On their left were the soldiers, the trappers held their right. The Sioux drive on the palisaded Arikara village carried home, protected though it was on the inside as well as the outside by ditches, and defended by some seven hundred warriors, many armed with rifles, but neither the soldiers nor the trappers did anything to support their friendly Indian allies. When the Sioux retired they brought with them a dozen or so 'Rees whom they had killed, and celebrated the night with a scalp dance. Col. Leavenworth was horrified by their barbaric ceremonies in which they dragged the bodies of the Arikara they had slain, and said so. The Sioux, on the other hand, it was clear, had done all the frontal attacking they intended to do and they had their own criticism of Leavenworth's tactics. If the 'Rees were dislodged they would join in the chase. For the present they looted the Arikara cornfields and other property they could get at, and withdrew. Col. Leavenworth now decided to make an attack without the Sioux. He fired a couple of shots from his cannon with excellent effect. The trappers advanced firing into the village until they were within ten feet of the palisades, and, finding that neither the soldiers nor the cannon supported them, they, too, withdrew. The trappers were, very naturally, furious. Col. Leavenworth then decided to make peace. He summoned the 'Ree chiefs to a pow-wow, in which they agreed to return the property they had stolen from Ashley's trappers. This was found to be merely a ruse. Col. Leavenworth and the united force now decided that they must really fight. When operations began the morning following the decision, they found the village empty, every Indian man, woman and child having slipped off silently during the night!

Andrew Henry, Bill Sublette, Jedediah Smith, Thomas Fitzpatrick, Edward Rose appear on the list of officers Col. Leavenworth had named at Ashley's suggestion as in command of the trappers. Bridger, the youngest of the trappers, was still a tenderfoot. He had shown himself a good fighter, capable of taking orders and carrying them out faithfully.

The fiasco at the Arikara village, however, had its lesson for young Jim Bridger, and one he

took to heart: a teetering uncertainty never char-
acterized his dealings with the Indians, either
in making a friendly advance or in stripping for
a fight.

# CHAPTER III

## BEAR, BANNOCK AND BEAVER TRAIL

ON their return journey to Fort Henry, five days out, the 'Rees, who were hovering on their flanks, fell on the Ashley-Henry party, killing two men and wounding two others, but the journey is memorable chiefly for the frontier's most famous and wierdest bear story. It is even more famous than the Mike Fink yarn, but unlike it, there are so many contradictions in the Hugh Glass story that it is difficult to determine the exact facts.

Hugh Glass was a hardy, seasoned veteran, employed as official hunter to the party. The

day following the 'Ree attack, he was out hunting with another member of the party, when a
grizzly suddenly loomed up in front of them.
Both men fired instantly, but failed to bring the
bear down.    Infuriated, the grizzly charged on
them.    Glass called on his companion to run
towards a bluff about a hundred yards behind
them.    A thicket in their path slowed them up,
and the bear was able to gain on them as its
great weight crashed easily through the brush.

With the bear at his heels, Glass tripped on a
stone and fell.    There was no time to get on his
feet, but enough to draw his pistol and fire into
the grizzly's face, to draw his knife and put up
the fight of his life as the bear struck and clawed.
Glass's companion, unnerved by what had happened so suddenly, ran back to the party and
reported that the old hunter had been killed.

Major Henry secured two volunteers from his
men, a veteran and a youngster, and asked them
to see that Glass was properly buried.    When
these men arrived on the scene they found the
bear lying dead over the hunter, with twenty
knife wounds and three bullets in his body.
Glass, although his flesh had been torn in strips,
and strewn on the ground near by, his scalp
wrenched and hanging over his face, was still
breathing.

The stories differ greatly as to the subsequent actions of these two men. One states that they, feeling it was impossible for Glass to live and being unwilling to bury him alive, gathered up his rifle and equipment, which was, of course, of great value in the wilderness, went back to the party and reported that they had buried Glass. Other versions say that these men stayed five days with the hunter before they abandoned him. If this is true the hazard of the rescuers' vigil must have been great for it began the day after the party had been attacked by the Arikaras on the march, and it was probable that they were still in the vicinity. Two men forced to stay in one place would have been just the sort of easy picking Indian stalkers would have enjoyed.

In any case Hugh Glass was a long way from dead. The two men left him, according to one story, his knife, flint, steel and tinder. The hunter's first meal was on the grizzly. When he plucked up sufficient strength he crawled, living on such roots, berries and fruit as he could find, until he fell in with some friendly Indians. There he recovered so fast that he was able in the course of a few weeks to rejoin the Ashley-Henry trappers.

Naturally enough, the drama of the story turns on Hugh Glass confronting the men who had abandoned him, and many imaginations have worked on getting the most out of the situation. He is supposed to have met the younger of the two men first, who was dumbfounded and thought he was seeing a ghost. Glass readily forgave him, but the other man, when the hunter met him, is reported to have been conscience-stricken, to have fallen on his knees and begged for mercy. There was, as we have seen in the Mike Fink story, no law in these wilds. Each man settled his own quarrels in his own way. The men were themselves a mixture of some of the finest characters known in our frontier history, as well as some of the roughest and toughest of any period or clime.

None of the published accounts mentions Bridger's name in connection with this incident, but there is a tradition that Jim was the youngster of the famous Hugh Glass story. It is impossible now either to prove or disprove that tradition. It is not impossible that Bridger the tenderfoot deserted Glass. Courage, loyalty, other qualities we greatly admire, are not born in us. We acquire them, sometimes through bitter experiences. *If* Bridger ran away from Glass he redeemed himself a thousand times over before his days on the trail were ended.

The main Ashley-Henry party had no sooner

reached the fort than a party of Blackfeet attacked them, killed four men, and looted them of twenty-two horses. The leaders were now forced to take stock of their position. It was more than sixteen months since the expedition had set out. Still on the beaten trail they had lost thirty or forty men, some of them seasoned veterans on whom they could depend, a large quantity of supplies, and a number of valuable horses. They had been driven back from their one attempt to advance up the Missouri, and now the Blackfeet were challenging the tenure of even their fort. The loss of the horses made it more difficult than ever, if not impossible for them to continue up the Missouri into the country of the hostile Blackfeet.

In this predicament Rose—one of the men whom we have mentioned as having been named by Col. Leavenworth as an officer—came to their rescue. Edward Rose was another one of the remarkable characters of this frontier. Very few of the men who have written the history of these times have had a good word for him, Washington Irving in his Astoria and The Adventures of Captain Bonneville has no hesitation in referring to him as "an outlaw and a designing vagabond." Rose, who had some negro blood in him, had been a pirate in the days when they were an institution outside New Orleans. He was known as Cut-Nose, from a saber cut that disfigured his face.  In the western wilderness he had been adopted by the Crow Indians, and won his place among them as a sub-chief. Even Irving was forced to pay tribute to the bravery that had gained Rose his place in the Indian tribe.  He had won his spurs with the Crows in war against their traditional enemy, the Blackfeet.  Once when the Blackfeet had fortified themselves behind a barricade and the Crows stood by undecided whether to attack or to retreat, Rose had shamed them into following him by leaping into the barricade, shooting one Blackfoot with his rifle, then wresting a war club from an enemy warrior striking down four others in quick succession.

Cut-Nose Rose had already served Ashley well in the Arikara matter; he now led Henry (while Ashley returned to St. Louis) southwest along the Yellowstone to a friendly encampment of the Crows at the junction of the Powder River.  Here the trappers were able to replenish their stock with the purchase of forty-seven horses.  The plan of proceeding up the Missouri was now entirely abandoned.  Andrew Henry continued along the Yellowstone, but he detached various parties to follow the tributary streams.

One such party under the command of Etienne Provot, and consisting among others of Jim Bridger, was detailed to trap the Powder River and its branches. These men followed the Powder into its source in the mountains, then crossed the Continental Divide into the Sweetwater, followed it westward, then turned back along the Green, and recrossed the divide, coming through the mountains by a great saddle, a place so broad that twenty wagons could be driven abreast, the only one of its kind in the Rockies. Its crest was reached, coming up from the east, with so gradual a rise that it was difficult to tell when the summit had been reached.

It was the South Pass, or, as the trappers called it, the Southern Pass, destined for fame as the mountain crossing of the Oregon and California emigrant trains.

The pass became so famous that a great many claims were put forward to its discovery, few of them having any merit. In the late forties a Missouri newspaper man claimed that Fitzpatrick discovered the pass, but at a later date than that given here. General Dodge, who credits the discovery to Bridger but places it in 1827, follows a long accepted mountain and plains tradition that Bridger was the first white man to find it, and Mr. J. Cecil Alter, who made a study of all the records available, feels that it is most reasonable to believe that the South Pass was discovered by Bridger during this journey.

Since Bridger, rather than Provot who was in command of this party, was credited with the discovery, it is likely that Jim came upon it while scouting ahead of the party. The keen observation and ability to find his way unfailingly in great stretches of country, was already showing itself, though Bridger had yet much to learn before those powers were brought to their full development.

The Provot-Bridger party after they had come through the Pass picked up the Big Horn River and followed it back to the Yellowstone River. If their course is traced on a map as we have outlined it, it will be seen that the party traveled at a rough estimate twelve to fifteen hundred miles during this fall hunt. If we add about half that distance for ground covered by different members of the party in following tributary streams, and an equal distance covered by scouting parties surveying the country before the main party advanced, one gets an idea of the vast territory the entire expedition was able to cover in three or four months.

Other parties had moved west, east and south. It was only necessary to put the knowledge gained by these various parties together to see that a new way into the mountains had been opened up. Possibly this was the first thing they did when the parties came together for their winter encampment. It was great news and a hurry message was sent to Ashley to catch him if possible before he set out with the year's supplies. Winter traveling was no easy thing and a seasoned, hardy veteran was chosen for the task —no less a person than Hugh Glass! Setting out in January, the sturdy old hunter followed the Powder River, crossed over to the Platte, where he built bull-boats and floated downstream to the Missouri and St. Louis.

In the meantime, as soon as spring opened the streams again, the expedition broke up into three parties. One moved northward into Montana; another into the country we call Utah; a third trapped up the Big Horn, south across Wyoming and the waters of the Green River. In nine months after abandoning Fort Henry the whole complexion of the enterprise had changed. The spring catch of furs was excellent and Henry himself, following the route by which he had entered the new country, took the catch of furs down the Yellowstone and Missouri Rivers to St. Louis. Good time could be made going downstream. It was possible to average fifty or sixty miles a day using dug-out canoes, bull-boats or flatboats. That was the last the mountains saw of Andrew Henry; he never returned to them again. He was nearly fifty years of age; he had been among the very first trappers to adventure into the mountains. The life was strenuous; it was a young man's world; and there were many leaders coming up to take his place.

For us here, this year—1824—is chiefly memorable for Bridger's discovery of Great Salt Lake. Two members of his party, trapping the Bear River, fell into an argument as to the course followed by that turbulent stream. Bridger offered to settle the dispute by finding out. He built a bull-boat, after the Indian pattern. It was a simple and handy way of traveling down the mountain streams and rivers, but useless for propulsion; it could not be rowed or paddled. It was put together in a few hours. Willow, birch or any flexible wood was used to make the frame work—circular in shape, with a round bottom—consisting of a criss-cross of pliable saplings or branches. Green buffalo hide was then stretched over it and smoked, the seams caulked with buffalo fat, and bound to the frame work by thongs. It was a buoyant craft, sturdy enough to stand a considerable bouncing against rocks in rough water, and so light that a squaw could lift it off and carry it out of the water. Bridger pushed off in such a craft, bounced through the canyon, and slipped into quiet water in the valley. He climbed a mountain to get a good view of the country and found that before him stretched an immense body of water, whose further end reached the horizon. Returning to his boat, Bridger went down the stream and a little way into the lake. He tasted the water and found it was salt. When he returned to the party and reported what he found, they thought it was an arm of the Pacific. Two years later a party was sent to explore it and find out what beaver streams flowed into it.

The following year, 1825, wandering alone in the high mountains in what is now the southeast boundary of Yellowstone Park—a place whose mystery fascinated him and continued to fascinate even after he had explored every one of its wonders—Bridger came on Two Ocean Pass and some of the other phenomena of that region.

Very few of Ashley's trappers shared this desire of Bridger's, already so strongly marked, to explore. The trapper was interested in the beaver and followed the streams. Bridger was developing along other lines also. Soon his fellows were to speak of him as one of the ablest hunters and trappers that ever lived in the mountains. He was coming up too as a leader, sharing with Fitzpatrick in the command of parties directed to trap certain sections.

He was learning the ways of the mountains and of the Indian. These early years are a checkerboard of Indian forays, against individuals and against whole parties. Provot, after whom the Utah city is named, while in that country, lost seven men in a Snake attack. There were one or two small scraps with the Crows. The Blackfeet were becoming interested, and had already stolen a number of horses. Other Indians, too—the Utes, Bannocks and others, kept a hostile eye on the moving trappers.

In an incredibly short time, however, the whole business of these American trappers was set and molded into an institution. Ashley sent word in the spring of 1825 that he would bring the supplies right into the trapping grounds. He packed in all the supplies they needed,— guns, traps, sugar, coffee, flints, powder, lead, tobacco, whisky; Indian trade stuff such as beads, mirrors, vermilion, bright cloths,—on horses and mules. It was a piece of enterprise that was to reap a harvest. Instead of making long jour-

neys to trading posts, free-trapper and Indian
had what they needed brought to their door, and
a market for their furs as well. There were eight
hundred people present at the first rendezvous.
The wilderness market lasted only one day, so
rapidly was the business disposed of. The place
where this first mountain fair was held is to-day
known as Bridger Flat.

Ashley was endowed both with personal courage and fearless enterprise, and his reward was
well-merited. He took back with him after the
first rendezvous one hundred and ninety-one fur
packs worth about a thousand dollars each, and
an equally good haul the next year.

Ashley married in 1825 and wanted to retire
from the mountains. He had amassed a small
fortune, and he sold out to three young men who
had helped him to it, receiving sixty thousand
dollars from Jedediah Smith, David Jackson
and William Sublette for the business that he
had established. At the 1826 rendezvous he
made a touching speech to the trappers who had
served him, assuring them of his interest in them
and of the friendly tie that had bound them
through so many hazards.

But long before this rendezvous and Ashley's
leaving-taking, young Jim Bridger had graduated from the tenderfoot class. When Ashley

gave up his business Bridger was just over twenty-two.  He was marked as a leader; the young
trappers referred to him as "Captain" Bridger,
the older men spoke of him affectionately as
"Old Gabe."  His graduation exercises might
well be considered—as indeed they were to mark
the new kind of relations the trappers were to
have in the future with raiding Indians—as taking place in a little encounter with the Indians.

Horse-raiding was a popular Indian sport.
Its inconvenience to the trapper who had to continue his business, as we have seen, was immense,
if indeed it did not actually strand the white men
in the wilderness.  Indians usually conducted
these forays on foot, slipping into the herd, fling-
ing themselves on horses and driving the whole
band to their villages.  It was a game they felt
that only an Indian knew how to play.

A party of Bannock Indians stole into the
trappers' camp, and ran off eighty horses.  Forty
volunteers were called for among the trappers,
Bridger and Fitzpatrick put themselves at their
head, and followed the trail of the horses to the
Bannock village.  Plans were rapidly made.
Fitzpatrick with a group, advanced on the camp,
firing as they came.  Bridger taking a few men
slipped into the Indian horse herd, and cut three
hundred of the animals loose.  It was impos-

sible, of course, for such a few men to get away with so large a number of horses, and a great many of them were lost.  Six Bannocks lost their lives in the fighting, while not a single one of the trappers received a scratch, the trappers coming back to camp in triumph with twice as many horses as the Indians had stolen.

The reason we choose that incident to mark Bridger's coming of age is this: In playing the Indian's game he was showing a certain conceit that had been developing in him.  As tender-foot, mountain man, trail-breaker and scout he cared little for fame, for wealth or the many other things in which our pride finds solace. Jim Bridger's single conceit was this: he hated to think that there was anything Indians could do at which he could not outdo them.

# PART II

## Mountain Man

## CHAPTER IV

### YOUNG MEN TO THE FORE

THE Ashley-Henry expedition had been a venture in trapping for furs. The territory into which it drifted was an accident. A number of discoveries had resulted which were to play an important part in subsequent history.

General Ashley had no idea when he packed in the supplies on horses and mules in 1825 and had his first rendezvous or mountain fair, that he was providing the one essential to creating a new type of pioneering American, the Mountain Man, the men who lived their lives, not merely trapped or hunted in the mountains. A few bold trappers and explorers had ventured into parts of the mountain region, and a number of these seasoned hunters were among Ashley's men. But despite the advantage they had in skill and experience, the leaders of the new era came not from their ranks but from the ranks of Ashley's younger men. Smith, the Sublette boys, Fitzpatrick, Jackson and Bridger—the youngest of the group—were to so improve their knowledge of the country by systematic exploration, by labor saving assignments, and especially offensive tactics against the Indian, that groups of even the fiercely independent free-trappers were forced, at the rendezvous or on the trail, to put themselves under the command of these leaders.

It was fair enough, for before the coming of Ashley's men it was almost a mathematical certainty that any small group of trappers trying to maintain themselves even on the outskirts of these mountains for any length of time would inevitably be driven out by the Indians, whereas in this new day that begins with Bridger as its most shining light, a small group of men kept themselves continuously in the field, heavily outnumbered though they were by every Indian tribe in the vicinity, while they followed the beaver with impunity wherever the fur-trail might lead.

The new arrangement was one that worked an advantage all round. The aristocrats among the men belonging to one of these Rocky Mountain Fur Company (that was the name of the company though in its earlier years it was little used) groups were the free-trappers, who took service with them both because men like Bridger soon became *the* experts in the knowledge of the best beaver country, and because of the security their commands provided in hostile country. The free-trapper either turned in his catch at a settled rate to the company, or paid the company a certain amount, usually about forty dollars a season, for the privilege of making himself a part of the company's encampment. Next came the skin-trappers, who worked on a set rate for the furs they turned in; then other trappers paid a regular wage. About one-third were men employed to do the work around the camp. As they gained experience the hunters moved from one class to the other.

Beaver trapping was an occupation that called for a great deal of skill. Men like Bridger could glance at a stream and tell the number of beaver that would be found there. Beaver sign was a lore in itself that was often followed from a tree, miles from a stream, that had been felled for food by the sharp teeth of this interesting animal. Beavers made long journeys to do this sometimes. An expert followed such sign like a hound dog on scent.

An old Crow Indian chief, who liked the white men, once said that the two cleverest people in the world were the white man and the beaver. There was an instinctive cunning about the beaver, once his suspicion was aroused. He neatly turned the traps over or avoided them. The expert trapper used nice judgment in deciding whether the stream he was working contained beaver that were "wise" or not and suited his tactics to the conditions he found.

If it was a stream that had never been worked, or one that had not been trapped for a long while the routine was comparatively simple. The trapper chose the most likely spots, set his trap in the bed of the stream in shallow water, and chained it to a stake to which a float was attached. Directly above the trap, but out of the water, was hung the beaver "medicine." This was extract from the beaver's castor gland, rubbed on a twig or a stick. Both the Indian and the white man valued this beaver castoreum highly. To the former it was "strong medicine"; in the white folk's cities it was turned into patent medicines that were offered as cures for every ailment from a headache to the most serious afflictions.

The beaver followed his inquisitive nose to
the pungent odor of the medicine and in sniff-
ing up at it, put his hind feet into the trap. If
the stake held he drowned himself in a few minutes in turning over and over with the trap in
his struggles. If he managed to jerk it loose, he
usually dragged it into deep water before he was
exhausted. In that case the float stick marked
the position of the trap, and the trapper had to
dive in and recover it. This was cold work, as
traps which were set towards night had to be
examined in the morning. In addition, trapping
was a spring and fall occupation, with snow falls
in September when the fall hunt began; and half
frozen streams in March when the spring hunt
started. The trapper, therefore, looked with
care to his trap stake, which was as sturdy a stick
as he could find; and he drove it firmly into the
bed of the stream. The trapper made sure in
setting his trap that not a trace of human odor
was left anywhere near the trap, for the beaver's
sensitive nostrils would detect it instantly, and
the trap would be given a wide berth. This
meant that the hunter had to move up and down
the streams he wished to trap with his feet always in the water.

When beaver were "wise," quite different tactics had to be adopted. Their comings and go-

ings were studied, and traps set in runways and other likely places, where they would step into them accidentally. These mountain men studied the beaver so closely that they knew not only the animal's habits but his family relations. Almost at a glance they could tell the "bachelor" beaver, an unattached wanderer, whom they found it easier to take than the family beavers. The trapper was overjoyed when he came on a colony of these bachelors, for they sometimes collected in a group.

Although beaver was the most popular fur, the mountain men took with trap and gun many other skins; otter, racoon, fox, muskrat, buffalo, bear—any fur for which there was a market, the free-trapper scorning anything but the choice and expensive skins.

A free-trapper working by himself had to skin and prepare the beaver he caught; working with a group such as Bridger commanded, he turned in his beaver to the clerk, who credited him with five dollars or whatever was the prevailing rate, and the skinning and preparing and final packing were done by men in the camp who were employed for that purpose.

Not only did a good trapper, under this system, have more time to devote to the thing he was expert in, but his sense of security was im-

measurably increased.  Working alone or with
a small group, much of his time had to be given
to details of camping, skinning, preparing,
packing and other chores.  All of them had to
be done in the face of dangers to which he had
to be constantly alert.  Some of these the new
system saved him, although he had to do his
share in the big camp.  None of our frontiersmen in Indian country had to face quite the same
hazards from hostiles as these trappers had to
meet day after day.  An Indian scout from a
point of vantage, suspecting the presence of the
trapper, could watch the streams.  The trapper
had to stick by them.  Or the Indian scout could,
by sticking up his nose in the wind that swept up
or down the depressions that made the stream
beds, smell a camp fire a couple of miles away.
A trapper had to move on foot up and down the
streams, so that a watchful Indian had a chance
to steal his horse, or to rob his traps when he
moved away from them.  Not that it was as
easy as that—not by a long way, for these veterans were wise, and made every bird and animal tell them the story of lurking Indians.

These dangers were, of course, just as menacing when working with a large group as with a
small, but with this difference: With the small
group, if the men made a stand it would be

against crushing odds; if they ran for it, the run would be almost endless. Attached to a company such as roamed the country under Bridger's command, the trapper could send up a signal and run for the camp. If he was forced to fight, trappers from a dozen directions might come to his aid. If it was a really serious affair, the camp they fell back on would be one that was picked for just such emergencies, with some shrewd leader, daring or careful as the occasion might require, from whom to take their cue. By day, working in this way, there was a natural far-flung scout screen. Horses were hobbled and grazed under the eye of a guard; at night they were corralled. On the whole there was a healthy assurance that a raider would not take them unawares. Trappers in these commands usually worked in twos, the leaders—Bridger made a constant practice of this even when he was a captain—trapping with the others. Sometimes, depending on the country they were in, the trappers moved a great distance from the main camp, or were detached in small parties to work up and down streams or to explore a region.

On the trail, at the rendezvous or at the winter encampment, a rigid discipline was maintained by these commands. If anybody shirked

his share of camp duty, the "Boushways" or captain (boushways is the French word *bourgeois*
meaning a person of the middle class or shop-
keeper. The French rivermen used it to desig-
nate anybody who employed them; the trappers
used it to denote the man at the head of a trapping party) would ask those around how much
the task was worth. A sum would be named and
credited to the person then assigned to do the
job, an equal amount was charged against the
man who had failed to do the work. Rifles and
ammunition were frequently inspected. In an
Indian alarm there would be no commands, but
each man would know his part and proceed to
do it.

We have been anticipating our story somewhat, for much of this trail and camp practice
was developed in the years that followed, although the foundations were already laid when
Smith, Jackson and William Sublette took over
Ashley's company. These three men made an
excellent team, supplementing each other's abili-
ties in the conduct of the business. Smith was
the explorer, Sublette handled the supplies, and
Jackson took charge of the trapping. It was a
rare combination of public-spirit and scientific
interest, practical ability and good business
sense. Bridger's contract with Ashley to spend

three years in his trapping expedition had run
out, and he was free to do whatever he chose.
But the mountains had already cast their spell
on him, and although he was only twenty-two,
he was plainly marked as a leader, with a natural gift of remembering every place he saw, if
only once, and the instinct of a born topographer.  These made him, apart from the ability
he had developed as hunter, trapper, and Indian
fighter, extremely valuable, and the new company employed him, as they did Fitzpatrick and
the other young leaders; on what terms we do not
know.  Smith, Jackson and Sublette kept the
company only four years, as Ashley had done,
before handing it on, but in that period Bill Sublette and Smith did some remarkable things.

Sublette was at this time about twenty-seven
years old, a sandy-haired, blue-eyed giant.  He
was a Kentuckian, whose grandfather had lost
his life in Boone's wilderness.  His family had
migrated to St. Louis four years previous to the
Ashley expedition.  He as well as his brothers
were the traditionally excellent Kentucky
marksmen; resourceful in any situation; brave,
like every one of these mountain leaders, to the
point of a fault; kindly and courteous, ready at
any time to give a stranger a hand.

At this period all this vast country, from what

is now New Mexico and Arizona, north through all the Mountain States, and California, was Mexican territory. To the northwest there was a great tract of land marked on the maps as Oregon. The British Hudson Bay Fur Company regarded this as their special territory, their own trapping brigades working south and frequently coming in touch with the Americans. Sublette's first act as company head was to take some supplies that he had left over after the summer fair into the Snake River country and trade it for furs with the Flathead and Blackfeet who were under the Hudson Bay Company's influence. The following year coming in with supplies he brought a cannon—a four-pounder—a gift from General Ashley, that was set up in a fort that had been built near what is now Ogden, Utah. This was the first wheeled vehicle to roll along the great trail. Two years later—1830—Sublette made history by bringing in the year's supplies by wagon train, using fourteen vehicles for the purpose. He and his partners made a report of what they had done to the then Secretary of War, saying: "This is the first time that wagons ever went to the Rocky Mountains; and the ease and safety with which it was done proved the facility of communicating overland with the Pacific Ocean; the route from the

Southern Pass, where the wagons stopped, to the Great Falls of the Columbia, being easier and better than on this side of the mountains, with grass enough for horses and mules, but a scarcity of game for the support of men."

Jedediah S. Smith had a very different background from the Sublettes'. He was a year older than William Sublette—a little over twenty-eight—when he became part owner of Ashley's company. He was born in a little New York upstate town called Bainbridge, one of a family of thirteen children. He had as a youngster drifted to the Great Lakes and from there to St. Louis, where in 1824 he joined Ashley. He was deeply religious, and a letter written by a trapper concerning the Arikara engagement to which we have referred in an earlier chapter says that when one of the men killed was buried, Jedediah Smith conducted the funeral services, and made a "powerful prayer." He was even then a marked leader, being named as an officer of the trappers in the subsequent engagement, and his pluck in volunteering to take the message to Fort Henry through country he did not know, is outstanding. There is a passing reference to his being mauled and severely injured by a bear that fall on the Powder River.

Now, taking over the job of explorer-partner

of the new company—neither he nor Sublette forgot to make their separate departments pay— he set out from the rendezvous in August 1826 with fifteen men to Utah Lake, and went on following the Virgin River, through the Mohave desert to San Diego, California; northward then three hundred miles to the San Joaquin and Merced Rivers where he wintered. Starting back in May with only two men, and taking seven horses and two mules, he crossed the still frozen Sierra Nevadas, and reported at the rendezvous. Directly that was over he set out again for California with nineteen men, following the Colorado River. He lost ten men in an Indian attack, but pushed on into the California settlements, where he was thrown into jail by the Mexican authorities at San Jose and Monterey, but managed to bring enough of influence to bear to get himself out. The Mexican government released him, but with a warning to stay out of the country. Picking up the men he had left behind earlier in the year, he pushed northward, wintering on the way, and moving up during the spring into Oregon. On the Umpqua River Indians attacked his camp while he was out, and he came back just in time to find eighteen of his men killed and the entire fur pack looted. He headed for Fort Vancouver, where the head of the Hudson Bay Company, Dr. John McLoughlin, sent to the Indians who had attacked his camp and recovered his entire fur pack, paying him twenty thousand dollars for it. Smith reëntered the mountains by the northern route, and made one other long trip northward before he was to give up direction of the company's affairs.

He was planning to publish a geography and map of the western country, when he was killed in 1831 in a Comanche ambush on the Santa Fe trail. On the Cimarron desert, the train which he, Sublette and Jackson were taking, ran out of water. Smith pushed on ahead to reconnoiter. Finding a dry steam bed, he dug into it to get at the moisture he knew would be there, when the Indians brought him down mortally wounded. Game to the end, he used his rifle on the first warrior rushing to take his scalp, and killed a second with a ball from his pistol. Bill Sublette could find no trace of him. These details were learnt from Indians. It should be remembered that Jedediah Smith crossed and recrossed the mountains into California some fifteen years before General Fremont made the journeys which were to earn him the title of the Pathfinder.

Bridger's discovery of the South Pass, Ashley's pack train by what was to be substantially the Oregon Trail, Sublette's demonstration of the feasibility of the wagon train, Smith's pioneering the trail into California and Oregon—in seven years the trappers had set the whole scene for our great western adventure.

## CHAPTER V

### HOME TO THE MOUNTAINS

JIM BRIDGER'S services to the Smith, Jackson, Sublette Company was largely in carrying on the main business of trapping, moving as usual in command of a brigade, through vast tracts of country. One spring he guided Smith to Tongue River and Big Horn across the mountains. But the really memorable thing that happened to him, and that for us marks a milestone in his development, is the rather prosaic fact that following the rendez-vous of 1828 he accompanied the fur train to St. Louis, arriving there in time to spend his first

Christmas in a settled community since he had set out on his adventure six and a half years previous. St. Louis was home to Jim Bridger, and he had doubtlessly looked forward to his return there. He had set out a penniless youngster, now there was probably a thousand dollars or two in the pockets of his worn buckskins.

Physically, too, he was transformed. The natural gawkiness of a boy of eighteen had given place to a figure in which every muscle was set. The ruddy glow on the cheek of a semi-outdoors boy of the settlements had been supplanted by a skin that was baked, tanned and weathered in sun, wind, rain, snow and freezing cold of the mountains. His eyes, frank, merry eyes of a humorful youngster, had been transformed, with pupils that would dilate and contract like a wild animal's. There was the same alertness also— of body and muscles set on springs, and released by a hair-trigger to any alarm. A resourcefulness, too, was there, for his reputation was already being marked as one who would, no matter what the situation might be, always land on his feet. A few years later a trapper described him in this way: "He's an animal that lights on his legs at every cast; he knows every creek in the mountains, and can smell his way where he can't see it."

In reality the Jim Bridger who had come home to St. Louis was another person. The life he had lived, its exhausting strain, its almost suicidal dangers, its difference in ideals, could not fail to remake him.

To-day that life he led seems unbelievable. Marches of three or four thousand miles each year, across mountains, through canyons, often through snow piled high on the trails, in weather freezing sometimes with arctic bitterness, or blistering with the summer sun, wading day after day in the icy streams to set his traps, living largely on jerked buffalo, with only two intervals in the gruelling round—the summer rendezvous, and the winter encampment.

In the following years many distinguished visitors were to witness this summer rendezvous, the annual mountain fair, and describe its romance, the charm of its settings, its gayety and abandon, and especially of those "game-cocks among the common roosters of the poultry yard," the free-trappers. That swaggering individual must have been a sight for sore eyes, for this is how Captain Bonneville described him to Washington Irving: "His hair, suffered to attain to a great length, is carefully combed out, and either left to fall carelessly over his shoulders, or is plaited neatly and tied up in otter

skins, or parti-colored ribbons. A hunting-shirt
of ruffled calico of bright dyes, or of ornamented
leather, falls to his knees; below which, curi-
ously fashioned leggins, ornamented with
strings, fringes, and a profusion of hawks' bells,
reach to a costly pair of moccasins of the finest
Indian fabric, richly embroidered with beads.
A blanket of scarlet, or some other bright color,
hangs from his shoulders, and is girt round his
waist with a red sash, in which he bestows his
pistols, knife, and the stem of his Indian pipe;
preparations either for peace or war. His gun
is lavishly decorated with brass tacks and vermilion, and provided with a fringed cover, occasionally of buckskin, ornamented here and
there with a feather. His horse, the noble min-
ister of the pride, pleasure, and profit of the
mountaineer, is selected for his speed and spirit,
and prancing gait, and holds a place in his esti-
mation second only to himself. He shares
largely of his bounty, and of his pride and pomp
of trapping. He is caparisoned in the most
dashing and fantastic style; the bridles and crup-
per are weightily embossed with beads and
cockades; and head, mane, and tail are inter-
woven with abundance of eagles' plumes, which
flutter in the wind. To complete this grotesque
equipment, the proud animal is bestreaked and

bespotted with vermilion, or with white clay, whichever presents the most glaring contrast to his real color." Other pen pictures show the free-trapper with scalps taken in battle adorning his buckskins.

To the rendezvous came, too, the friendly Indian tribes, with pelts they wanted to trade; the Indian braves and Indian belles putting up a display of their own to rival the free-trapper.

Tests of skill and strength were naturally the order of the day. There were wrestling matches, horse and foot races, and shooting matches. Occasionally some quarrel led to men pacing off and settling the matter with their rifles. (In the civilized world gentlemen were then still settling some of their disputes with pistol or sword at dawn.) In many instances this was little more than a suicide pact with riflemen as expert as these trappers. It was at one of these gatherings a few years later that Kit Carson had his famous duel with the Frenchman Shumar, who broadcast a challenge after many contemptuous expressions directed at the Americans. The duelists rode towards each other, charging in like knights in an old world tournament, and holding their fire until the horses nearly touched. The ball from the Frenchman's pistol grazed Kit's head; Carson hit his man on the arm, the bullet passing up into his shoulder, and convincing Shumar that he had all the fight he wanted with an American trapper.

The games were preliminaries, to while away the time waiting for the supply train. When it arrived, and bales were ripped open, the real business of the fair began. Men who had gone through the almost fantastic hardships of a year on the trail, now threw away what they had earned with a prodigal hand. Free-trappers often spent as much as a thousand dollars, buying things for an Indian wife or an Indian belle whose fancy they aimed to catch, for necessary supplies, and for liquor. The liquor was bootleg stuff. Sale of spirits was prohibited in the Indian country, but traders were allowed a certain amount for their boatmen. First as whisky, later as plain alcohol, this was brought into the mountains, where it was frequently sold at four dollars a pint. The quantity traded was only just enough for one furious drunk, in which Indian vied with trapper in blowing the lid off. The scene on the morning following would often be chaotic; broken heads and noses were gingerly stroked; there was a rueful stock-taking of the year's earnings vanished and often of a debt contracted that would have to be worked off.

For a leader like Bridger, the rendezvous brought a number of responsibilities. First, the safety of the camp, and the necessary precautions against an attack by hostiles must be made; second, the leaders would have to oversee the trading and get the fur packs ready for the return journey to St. Louis; third, the leaders would have to decide on the whole plan for the fall and spring trapping expeditions, and the place in which each party would go into its winter encampment. These men worked fast for they had to sign on their men and make long marches—it might be anywhere up to a thousand miles to the streams they were going to trap.

The winter encampment was an entirely different matter. Beaver would be snared until the moment the streams froze up, usually late in December. Then the trappers would march to a secluded valley, where game was plentiful, and where the mountains cut off the arctic weather and formed a spring-like oasis. In it the encampment was pitched, and there the business of laying up the year's supply of meat began. The good leader saw that enough buffalo meat was jerked for the year, the necessary skins secured and prepared, garments and moccasins made, and everything overhauled for the spring hunt. If game gave out, the encampment was moved. On the whole it was a period of relaxation and sport. Often as not, a friendly Indian tribe would pitch its encampment close by, and then there would be a good deal of rivalry in running the buffalo, in horse and foot racing.

The Indian was an inveterate gambler. In the long winter evenings he found opportunity for exercising this trait in a game that is variously called "Hand" or "Cache." It bears a strong resemblance to the game that white children play called "Who has the ring?" or "Hunt the thimble." The Indians divided into two groups. One side, to whom the lot fell, would take the sliver or stick that was to be hidden; it would be placed in the hands of one of the players; and it would be the business of the other side to guess who had it. Score was kept by sticks. Each wrong guess would mean a credit to the holding side. When a correct guess was made, the stick or sliver would be passed to the guessing side. The holding side always made a tremendous din, keeping up a continuous chant, shouting, beating on a drum. The side that secured a given number of credit sticks would be declared the winner, and gather up everything that had been wagered, a brave sometimes losing all he possessed in betting on the outcome of the game.

For a brigade leader such as Bridger, the protection of the camp continued to be a serious responsibility. Horses must be guarded. There were the usual rigid inspections of firearms, and other camp precautions. The encampments were also not without their serious side. A youngster named Osborne Russell who served in Bridger's command, says of his winter encampment: "The long winter evenings were passed away by collecting in some of the most spacious lodges, and entering into debates, arguments or spinning yarns until midnight, in perfect good humor, and I for one will cheerfully confess that I derived no little benefit from the frequent arguments and debates held in what we term 'The Rocky Mountain College,' and I doubt not that some of my comrades who considered themselves classical scholars, have had some little added to their wisdom in the assemblies, however rude they might appear."

The period was also a time in which Bridger had an opportunity to make a few lonely excursions. The area that we now know as Yellowstone Park fascinated him, and during the course of the years he was to examine almost every inch of it. His head had begun to carry a huge map.

Part of it he knew for himself and in it was set not merely every mountain, stream and ravine, but the tiniest details. Part he had learnt from others and carefully fitted into the picture, and when opportunity offered in this period of relaxation, he took the occasion to fill out some of the gaps. He did a great deal of winter wandering, despite the intense cold. Often it was so cold that to sit still on a horse was to freeze, but the world of the mountains in the winter had a new loveliness. The icicles on the evergreens irradiated a thousand lights when the sun shone on them, and many places then took on a fairyland charm. These lonely wanderings had a part in making Jim Bridger. He learned to live for long periods with no companionship except his own thoughts; his mind was steeled gradually until he was able to feel himself as part of the vast solitude. Some men have gone mad when forced into such loneliness; Bridger learned to plug on day after day by himself and actually enjoy it.

Lest our picture of the free-trapper convey the impression that it was also a portrait of Bridger, we hasten to say that there is no evidence whatever that he ever appeared in so extravagant a get-up. Young Bridger made no set at any Indian belle; responsibilities the free-

trapper did not know fell early on his shoulders;
we know that the swashbucklers looked down
on him because he was sober and frugal. All
the pictures we have of Bridger show him
dressed modestly. He wore skin garments in
the mountains, of course. They were warm; the
materials were at hand with which to make them.
His clothes in cold weather would more likely
have been a flannel shirt, or one made of buckskin; a pair of skin breeches; blanket or buffalo-
skin leggins; felt hat or cap of buffalo or otter
skin; moccasins of deer, elk or buffalo hide, with
long flaps that could be wound around the ankle,
and with pieces of blanket or fur in them to
take the place of stockings, and a heavy loose
coat of buffalo robe, or the Canadian capote,
which many trappers preferred to any other
overcoat. The capote was a coat with a hood
attached that could be pulled down over the
head. The one the trappers used is described as
having a warp nearly as coarse and strong as
fish-lines, and a woof of twisted beaver or other
fur with a very heavy nap.

His equipment would be equally simple. Six
beaver traps in a skin case. A blanket, an extra
pair of moccasins, and some skin to repair clothing and footgear. Two antelope or deer skins,
which could be used for making a pack if he had

to carry anything, and could also be used as an extra cover at night. They could be cut into strings, made into a tent, used for repair of garments or put to a hundred other uses. His powder horn and bullet pouch, slung across the left shoulder and under the right arm, had an attachment for carrying a knife. A box for the beaver medicine, and a whetstone, for the trapper's knife must always be kept at razor edge. A tobacco sack hanging around his neck would also carry a pipe and the flint and steel and tinder for fire making. The hatchet and pistol were carried at the belt; the rifle across the pommel of the saddle.

Accoutered thus, and with an emergency ration of pemmican—buffalo meat ground and mixed with fat—and an extra horse, Bridger learnt enough to sustain himself in the mountains indefinitely, or to make a march of any distance he might desire. It would be necessary for him only to replenish his supply of ammunition. With a little salt and sugar he would be living high, and both of these he knew how to find in the mountains, extracting the latter from the trees. The tenderfoot trying to live on a meat diet would as likely as not fall ill of scurvy. Bridger—the Bridger who returned home to St. Louis—was already mountain wise.

The bark of trees, edible plants, honey from the bee, with fresh meat and fish as he found them from time to time, would give him an all round well-balanced diet that would keep him as strong and fit after a three-thousand mile journey as the day he had set out.

The mountains, of course, had their peculiar dangers—snow slides, crevices, tumbling streams, steep hills, deep canyons, the fierce grizzly. These had their part in the making of Jim Bridger, for he had slowly to master all their lore. But it was the Indian, who not only made the life Bridger had known a continual hazard, but whose skill on warpath and trail was a trumpet blaring a challenge to Jim Bridger's ambition. They played so large a part in making Bridger that we must take a whole chapter to consider them.

Jim Bridger went home to St. Louis. What he did there we do not know. If his sister was still alive he had the means to make her a handsome little present. Old friends were probably visited, and a yarn or two spun of mountain wonders and Blackfeet fights. But it was a different Jim who had come back. The charm of the city was gone, once and for all, never to return.

When he set out in March of the following

year on his return journey with the supply train
and sixty new recruits he was making a second
home-coming journey. This time it was home to
the mountains. Henceforth there would be, on
rare occasions and as duty alone made necessary,
simply *visits* to the "settlements."

# CHAPTER VI

## "Injuns"

IT IS difficult to appraise the extent to which the Indian has influenced the American character, our daily lives, habits and practices. His corn and potatoes and tobacco have spread over the world. Do our college fraternities derive from his secret honor societies? Our pep meetings trace to the dance he indulged in before he took the warpath, our football victory snake dance from his celebrations of triumph? The frank inquisitiveness and the lavish fuss we make of foreign visitors—giving them frequently a wrong impression of both our regard and admiration—seems to have a counterpart in the manner in which the Indian received the white man. These typical American customs seem to have no root in our Anglo-Saxon inheritance, any more than the peculiar doggedness the American boy displays when he practices constantly the details of a game in which he wishes to excel. The patience with which a baseball enthusiast, for instance, will for long periods simply throw and catch a ball, seems to have no duplicate in any European character. Are the clean shaven faces of our men the result of the Indian's abhorrence of hair on the body?

Certain it is that the Indian profoundly influenced our ideas of warfare. Our backwoodsmen learned his tactics, and the effect, when our frontiersmen were engaged, as at New Orleans, was overwhelming against the European soldier trained on a barrack square. The Indian taught us how to live in the wilderness and set us on our first step towards conquering it. So superior was the Indian as a warrior that in the first encounters with colonial and American troops the result was simply a massacre of whites. Even after we learned to treat his tactics with respect the best our regulars could do in the early days was to exchange three or four men in combat for one Indian we killed. Backwoodsmen could bring that average down nearly to two to one, which was about the best showing we could make in the forest country. On the plains in pitched battles our troops with superior weapons and a better range for fire could not beat them with equal numbers. If the warlike tribes had been capable of united action and the ability to sacrifice themselves in the manner of white men for a common cause, outnumbered though the Indians were in the whole country from five to ten times even at the founding of the Republic, it is impossible to estimate what they would have cost us in blood and treasure.

Jim Bridger could not help but be profoundly impressed by the necessity of equipping himself to hold his own with the Indian. His first tenderfoot experiences had been humiliating. The Assiniboines and the Arikaras had fooled the Ashley-Henry party, stolen their horses, and killed a number of men. The Blackfeet had not only barred their way up the Missouri, but had nearly brought disaster on the enterprise by their attack on the fort. Later even so marked a leader as Jedediah Smith had lost seven-eighths of his men in his California and Oregon excursions. Before and after Bridger graduated from the tenderfoot ranks the menace of the raiding Indians was to keep him constantly on his mettle.

In the record made of the winter encampment

of 1826-27 by a man named Jim Beckwourth, who was fond of pointing out what a bear he was at killing Indians, there were no less than three raids by the Blackfeet, and one by the Bannock Indians, whom Bridger followed up with two hundred and fifteen trappers and drubbed severely. Beckwourth states that the raids made by the Blackfeet were in bodies of forty-four, two thousand five hundred, and five hundred, respectively, but these figures are probably a gross exaggeration, as are his figures of the numbers of Indians killed. His own encounters are so exaggerated that they are humorous. He says that during one of these raids he came across a party of ten Blackfeet and that he killed nine of them. In all he gives seven to eight hundred Indians killed by the trappers and scalped. At that rate there would not have been a hostile Indian left in the mountains in three years.

Unless trapped, Indians never took heavy losses. Their plans were laid on the basis of something for nothing. The loss of a single man was a matter of mourning to the whole tribe, and an ambitious brave anxious to prove himself as a leader found himself judged more in terms of the losses he suffered than in the scalps and horses he brought back. The significance of what Beckwourth says is that the raids had been made against an encampment of eight hundred trappers and friendly Indians. One can only imagine how persistently their trail was dogged when the trappers were broken up into smaller parties, and forced to scatter in their business of trapping the streams.

This man Jim Beckwourth was another one of those remarkable characters of the mountains. Like Rose he, too, seems to have had some negro blood. The trappers cared little what a man's antecedents were, and Beckwourth's pluck was highly valued by them. One of the trappers seeing a Crow chief notice Beckwourth's swarthy complexion, told the Indian that Beckwourth was in reality a Crow who had been stolen as a child from them by the Cheyennes. While Beckwourth the following spring was working a stream in company with Bridger, they turned up along separate forks, agreeing that the first to finish would cross over to the other. Bridger crossed the ridge that separated them just in time to see Beckwourth captured by a number of young Crow braves. Beckwourth was hurried to the chief, who sent for all the women of the village who had lost children in a Cheyenne raid many years ago. One of them said that if Beckwourth was her son he would have a mole under

his eyelid, and sure enough when it was turned
up a similar mark was found. Beckwourth, although he knew he was no Crow, took advantage of the coincidence, and stayed on with them,
proving himself in many a fight and becoming
a sub-chief of the tribe. He served the U. S.
army as a scout and guide in his later years.

Jim Bridger's Indians read like the roll call
of the tribes: the Arikaras, the Assiniboines, the
Sioux and Cheyennes in their many branches;
the Piegans, the Flatheads, the Nez Perces, the
Bannocks; the Iroquois of our first frontier,
brought here by the Hudson Bay Company;
William Penn's Delawares, among the fiercest
warriors now, having carved out a hunting
ground of their own in the west and making
war on every tribe; Boone's Shawnees; the Kansas, Rockaways and Winnebagos, the Arapahoes
and Pawnees. The lowly Digger, the Snake,
and the fierce Ute of the desert uplands; the
Comanche and Apache of the south, through
whose country Bridger journeyed; the Crows,
who in later years were to regard him as one of
their own chiefs. But foremost of all must stand
the Blackfeet, with whose enmity Bridger was
constantly to cope in these early years.

Blackfoot and Blackfeet are supposed to desig-
nate two branches of this tribe, related and

banded to other branches spoken of as the Gros
Ventres of the Prairies, Piegans, Bloods, etc.,
and referred to generally by one name or the
other. Their home grounds ran from Wind
River mountains in the south to the headwaters
of the Missouri in Montana, northward into
Canada, and covering nearly the whole of modern Montana north of the Yellowstone River.
The legend is that they got their name because
in one of their migrations they followed a great
prairie fire, and the Indians of the country into
which they entered, seeing their moccasins black-
ened, so named them. Another explanation is
that they used blackfurred skins in making their
moccasins, wearing them with the fur on the
outside.

They were, however, people "of the feet."
Most of their raiding, a great deal of their
hunting was done afoot, although they were excellent horsemen, riding a sturdy little mountain pony. They even ran the buffalo without
horses, usually in the spring, when the soft,
sticky ground slowed the shaggy beasts down
and allowed these Indian runners to come up
with them. Meriwether Lewis, during the
progress of the Lewis and Clark expedition,
killed a Blackfoot Indian, and from that moment the tribe was the sworn enemy of all

Americans. It was simply adding one more enemy to their list, for the Blackfeet were constantly at war with every tribe in their neighborhood, and they were ready to scrap with any others they might come across in the long journeys they made. They constantly raided the Crow, Bannock, Snake, Nez Perces and Flathead country. Every American trapper who had attempted to enter their country so far had been thrown back, small parties being extremely glad to retire with their lives. The Rocky Mountain Company's trappers had made a few incursions into that country but generally speaking left it alone. The Blackfeet traded with the British, being armed, when they had guns, with the Canadian smooth-bore fusee, as were the Canadian trappers. The American trapper despised this weapon, for nothing less than the accurate long rifle would satisfy him.

The Canadians, although they suffered occasionally from Blackfoot raids, did not regard them as their greatest enemy. That honor, if one might judge from the diary of Peter Skene Ogden, a partisan or captain in charge of Canadian trappers, they reserved for the Snakes, who on the whole were friendly to the Americans. Ogden suggested to some American trappers that they join in exterminating the whole Snake

tribe, so that we can easily believe that Indian
raids on their rivals was looked on by either
side with some indulgence.

As with other warring tribes, Bridger saw
that the whole Blackfoot system of warfare,
whether of attack or defence, was predicated on
good preliminary scout work. Against those
comparative noncombatants, the Nez Perces,
the Blackfeet needed nothing but a few scouts,
who would first watch the enemy encampment,
then crawl in silently, cut the horses loose, stampede the herd and the camp. With sturdier opponents, the scout work would assure them of
the correct moment to make the raid, for the
Indian attack tactics could be summed up in
one word, surprise. He only yelled when he
hoped to turn the resulting confusion into a
panic.

One of the favorite means the Blackfoot scout
used in open country to keep a camp or a body
of men under observation was to rig himself out
as an antelope, which both Indian and trapper
considered less desirable meat than the buffalo.
Bridger's own early interest in developing his
powers of observation must have been stirred by
the way these men made every bird and animal
pay tribute to them in information about what
was happening in their neighborhood, the tiny

signs on ground or tree that became to them
so full of meaning.

Their ambuscades were cleverly chosen.
When forced to stand and fight, if in the open
they dug a shallow trench in a few minutes—
women did this often while the braves were
fending off the attack. If cover was available
they entrenched themselves there in a manner
that provided their archers and riflemen a good
view, with the poorest possible target for their
opponents. They would slip out of a trap at
night with the silence of a wraith. Their sense of
hearing was brought to so fine a pitch that there
is a record of one of their scouts shooting an
arrow at the click of a rifle trigger and hitting
his man in the dark. In the winter they skimmed
over the country on their snow shoes "like birds,"
where other men and horses were floundering in
the deep snow. Trained from their earliest
youth to a warrior's life, horse stealing or the
taking of an enemy scalp was the young brave's
way of proving himself. He had an instinctive
gift of utilizing the best cover—rocks, depressions, trees. There is a story in these mountain
days of a Blackfoot advancing in attack rolling
a log in front of him for cover.

Only one advantage the white trapper had
before he learnt the Indian's arts. He had a

superior weapon in his rifle and with it he was a peerless shot, while the Indian never was on the whole anything but an extremely poor marksman; in addition his powder and his weapon were often inferior. In the sort of fighting they had to do in the mountains, however, the arrow was not without its advantage. Trained from the toddling stage to use the bow, they had both accuracy and speed; even a boy could shoot his arrows so that there was a continuous flight of them in the air. These could be fired faster than the rifle, but at any distance their slow flight as compared to a bullet, was not as effective. The trapper's great advantage was that in open country he could deliver a telling fire long before the Indian could get within range in which he could use his weapon.

For an Indian brave there were only three occupations worthy of a warrior—war, sport and hunting. Sport meant horse and foot racing, jumping and wrestling. Since these things played so large a part in the Indian's life, and young Bridger set himself the task of excelling them, it is more than likely that in his early days in the mountains he gave some of his summer and winter to these sports. We know that he had a Comanche race-horse of great speed and endurance, named Grohean, of which he was

very proud. Riding was an everyday necessity
and good horsemanship was a necessary distinction that every mountain man, and especially
leader, must have. Doubtless young Bridger
had been in many a race proving himself. Races
were usually a match—one man against another.
The two champions stripped Indian-wise to the
waist, and rode bareback with nothing but a
leather thong caught by a noose around the
horse's lower jaw with which to guide their
mounts. The course, lined with a shouting
throng of trappers, squaws, braves and papooses,
was any distance agreed on by the contestants, or
set by a chief, who would also act as judge.
Stamina and speed of foot we know Bridger had.

The supreme sport in hunting was running the
buffalo. These animals were, under certain conditions, extremely stolid. The professional
hunter whose business it was to kill buffalo for
meat could often approach a herd on foot, keeping down wind of them, and shoot them down
one after the other until they were finally
alarmed. This method was consequently called
"approaching." "Running" was quite another
matter. This was conducted on horseback. The
herd would be raced and the hunter, ranging
alongside a buffalo he had marked, would shoot
a bullet or an arrow into its flanks, a good shot

hitting the animal just behind the shoulder and passing through its lungs. It was a thrilling and dangerous sport—racing in a cloud of dust, the broken, uneven ground would have to be taken in the stride; the buffalo, especially when tired, began to fight, making quick, sudden jabs at the horse, which as quickly leaped aside. This called for a firm seat and a sure grip.

The number of buffalo brought down would depend entirely on accurate shooting and ability to reload. There was a great advantage in using the bow and arrow, for it could be shot much faster than the rifle, and the short bow the Indian used, delivered its arrows so powerfully at short range that cases are mentioned in which an arrow was known to pass completely through a buffalo. The mountain Indian's favorite bow wood was osage, to procure which he often made long journeys. The string was made of sinew. The bow was about four feet long and backed with sinews, resulting in a weapon of considerable stiffness, and an untrained person could scarcely spring it more than an inch or two. It delivered reed arrows with great speed. These were feathered two or three inches, with a head first of notched stone and later of iron. Its tremendous penetrating power was only at very close range, the arrows losing power quickly in flight.

Hunting buffalo with the muzzle-loading rifle or pistol depended for results on skill in reloading while on a running horse. The ramrod was carried sometimes attached to a loop hung around the neck. Frequently bullets were carried in the mouth. The powder once rammed in, the patched ball would be dropped into the barrel. To save time in driving it home against the powder, the use of the ramrod would sometimes be discarded. Instead, the butt of the gun would be stamped down against the pommel of the saddle. This was a dangerous practice, because if the blow failed to slide the bullet down, the powder would explode in an airtight compartment within the bullet-choked barrel, and a burst gun would often result. Pistol fire would be delivered only to the rider's right; rifle fire only to his left. The thundering herd, the dust, the racing horses, the shots all made for excitement. These affected the tenderfoot so seriously that the mountain men described it as "buck ague." An untried hunter was usually given plenty of elbow room, for tenderfeet were known to become so excited as to shoot their own horses without knowing what they were doing.

But Bridger was not content to learn to excel

the Indian only in his skill on the warpath, the sport and hunting trail. He set himself to understand the Indian's ways of thought, his beliefs, his ideals, his habits, his customs, and to master his languages. Before his days in the mountains were over he could talk more than a dozen of them well, and he knew the Sign Language as no white man did. He was the linguist among our scouts, for in addition to the Indian languages he learnt, he could speak Spanish and French as fluently as he did English.

It is difficult to-day to even form an estimate of the number of battles and raids with Indians Bridger survived. Each one of the trappers who made a record of his stay in the mountains has half a dozen different incidents in which Bridger was involved in scraps with various tribes. Every one of the figures of our western movement who came into the mountains or passed through it furnishes a revealing incident. Bonneville in '32 reports an incident in which Bridger received two arrows in his back; Dr. Marcus Whitman, on his journey to Oregon three years later cut out an arrowhead from his back. Rev. Samuel Parker says in his diary: "It was a difficult operation because the arrow was hooked at the point by striking a large bone and a cartilaginous substance had grown around it.

The doctor pursued the operation with great self-possession; and his patient manifested equal firmness."

That was in 1835, and the arrowhead was probably the one he received three years previously, but there can be no connection between them and what Father De Smet, the famous Roman Catholic missionary who first visited the mountains in 1841, has to say. Referring to Bridger in a letter he writes: "He had, within four years, two quivers full of arrows in his body." One army officer, in later years wrote that Bridger had three arrow wounds in his back; another, that he had several wounds, besides being hit so as nearly to break his neck. Probably before his course was run his body was scarred with bullet, arrow, knife and other wounds. His Indian fights cannot be counted; they must be reckoned in the hundreds; his wounds in the dozens.

It sounds fantastic, but that was the reason the men who knew him were indignant when in later years a comparison of his Indian adventures was drawn with those experienced by others, even such celebrated frontiersmen as Daniel Boone and Kit Carson. A dozen serious fights each year in these days in the mountains is a conservative estimate; when that is multi-

plied by the fifty active years Bridger spent in
the wilderness as mountain man, trail-breaker
and scout, one begins to realize the extent of
them. Much of it, and practically all the detail,
was lost with Bridger and the circle of men who
shared the hazards of that memorable life with
him.

When Bridger was nearly fifty, "The Adventures of Baron Munchausen" was read to
him. He was naturally amused by its humor of
exaggeration, bearing not a little resemblance to
the typical humor of the American backwoodsmen and still flourishing among our lumber men
and guides. Discussion of the book suggested
his own experiences. Referring to them he said
—this was the nearest he ever came to boasting
of his experiences:—that perhaps if his own adventures with the Blackfeet were set down on
paper they might seem equally improbable!

# CHAPTER VII

## AN OLD TRYST AND A NEW RIVAL

AT the summer rendezvous of 1830, the Rocky Mountain Fur Company was turned over to a new group of men. Ashley had kept the Company for four years, and then handed it on to the younger men, who had been its leaders. Smith, Jackson and William Sublette now, after having directed the company for the same period, handed it over in the same way to Fitzpatrick, Bridger, Milton Sublette, Henry Fraeb and Baptiste Gervais, for a consideration of thirty thousand dollars, with the important difference that William Sublette kept the business of handling the transportation department. The new partners were not the effective combination that the others had been. They could not be equaled as leaders in the field; but none of them had the business acumen of either Ashley or Bill Sublette.

Fraeb and Gervais, at the head of a small number of trappers, set out for the south, and the streams in what is now known as Colorado. Bridger, Fitzpatrick and Milton Sublette, now at last entire masters of their movements, decided on an entirely different course. As tenderfeet they had seen the Blackfeet bar Henry's way up the Missouri. That leader had turned southwestward into more friendly country, and the wilderness education of the new owners of the company had progressed at the expense of more than one humiliating experience of those raiders of the north. These youngsters were hard-bitten veterans now—not James Bridger, Thomas Fitzpatrick and Milton Sublette, but Old Gabe, Broken Hand, and Milt. Fitzpatrick was five years older than Bridger, who was now twenty-six. We have stressed the ages of these men because the leaders of the mountain men were not, as there has been a disposition to believe, "boy wonders." They were young men who served an arduous apprenticeship before they took their place as leaders.

Combining two hundred trappers in one command, Bridger, Fitzpatrick and Sublette, led them north—right into the heart of the Blackfoot country! It was a prime fur country, for these streams had been given a wide berth by the trappers. Crossing the Wind River Mountains to the Yellowstone River, they kept on north until they picked up Smith River, followed it to the Missouri, and turned down stream to Great Falls, where the Blackfeet had first barred their path.

From that point their action suggests that they were set on carrying out the plan Andrew Henry first had in mind. They followed the headwaters of the Missouri, down into the region that is now known as Yellowstone Park, trapping the Gallatin and the Madison, and following the streams eastward into a winter encampment in the Powder River country. A neat little fall journey of twelve or fifteen hundred miles in the course of less than five months, with trapping the everyday business. That in itself would be remarkable, but the miracle is that any one returned, for the journey, from the moment they entered the Blackfoot country, was one continuous battle.

Imagine the change that had taken place in the ability of these trappers, and we have the

clue to the fabulous character that Jim Bridger
became, for he was the field general and strate-
gist of these roving parties from now on. Andrew
Henry could not maintain himself with an equal
number of men on the edge of the Blackfoot
country; now Bridger had learned enough to
lead as small a party up and down the heart of
that country with impunity. His losses in men
were less than Henry had suffered while on the
beaten trail.

From here and there we gather some details
which show the manner in which Bridger
worked. The encampment, of course, was
chosen always with an eye to defence, the horses
always pastured under guard, and at night
corralled within the encampment. No Indian
party, of course, would dream of making an
open frontal attack on such a position, for losses
were a thing they were never willing to take.
While trapping, the camp became a natural cit-
adel for which the trapper could run on the first
alarm.

Bridger's first morning duty, when he rose at
dawn, would be to mount his horse and make a
great cast around the encampment. He grew so
expert at this that even from the back of a horse
thundering along at a gallop, his eye sweeping
the ground would infallibly read there the

MOUNTAIN MAN.

tiniest mark that a moccasin left.   Not one single man or horse could have crossed that circle
without his eye picking out the sign left.

It was the morning newspaper in which the
story of the night's doings was clearly written.
Everything would be noted—the passing of a
stray horse, a visit of wolves, the insects rousing
to work, the presence and action of the wild
game and birds, the scent lingering on the
ground, the direction of the wind and the smells
it bore.   If there was anything puzzling, its real
meaning would be carefully investigated.

If, near or far, "sign" of Indian was noted,
from some hill, using a telescope, Bridger would
carefully scan the entire country and the number of Blackfeet would be read by the number of
campfires, or by a dozen other indications when
their movement could not be plainly seen.   If
it was a large body, entrenchments might be dug
and barricades thrown up; if it was a small one,
the march would be resumed cautiously.

As the party moved, and it was a long line of
mounted men, with spare horses and equipment,
for some of the trappers took their Indian wives
with them, there would be a scout screen moving on high ground on both flanks, and front and
rear, and placed at so safe a distance that a signal
would give sufficient warning.   Defiles and

other points that looked like a good ambush would be carefully examined by the leader himself.

The Blackfeet realized that fall that they had something new to contend with, for they could not work that element of surprise, and without it their strategy was lost.

Coming out of their winter encampment, the party again headed for the Blackfoot country. The streams were full of beaver, and spring furs were always better and more valuable than the fall crop. They must have been rather cocky over their last excursion, for in crossing the Crow country, they became careless and a band of Crow warriors ran off three hundred of their horses. This was a good part of their stock, and the loss crippled the entire plans for the spring hunt.

But Bridger and his men were by now equal to almost any situation. Calling for a hundred volunteers he took the Crow trail on foot and followed it a hundred miles in two or three days, and came upon the rustlers at dusk. The horses were tethered in a corral with sixty or so young braves guarding them, but two of the trappers crept in, cut the horses loose and stampeded them, while the rest opened fire on the Indians, killing seven before the survivors melted into the night.

Somewhere along these earlier years Jim Bridger had become marked by the Indian tribes. They spoke of him as Casapy, the Blanket Chief. Why we do not know. Such knowledge would be interesting, because of the Indian habit of naming a person on account of some outstanding characteristic. Perhaps Bridger wore the Canadian blanket coat or capote, continually, and was so marked by them. Although for many years a junior in the mountains, Bridger seems to have been marked by the Indians as the trapper leader.

Fitzpatrick left the party to go down to St. Louis and escort the supply train, while Bridger and Milton Sublette pushed on into the Blackfoot country, making much the same journey as they did in the fall, and, incidentally, taking a good catch of furs. Last fall the Blackfeet had challenged nearly every foot they traversed; this spring their journey was almost unmolested.

Bridger and Milton Sublette coming down from the Blackfoot country to the summer rendezvous, learnt that something had gone wrong with the supply train. A rescue party was sent out, which came up with Fitzpatrick. He had been delayed through accompanying Bill Sub-

lette and Smith on the Santa Fe trail—this was
the occasion on which Smith was killed—and
had come up north through the country we now
speak of as Colorado.

But much worse than this delay was facing
the new company at the rendezvous. A powerful rival had come into the field. John Jacob
Astor, as you will remember, had made a pio-
neer bid for this fur trade, sending one party by
sea around the Horn, another overland, which
had led to the founding of Astoria, the entire
enterprise collapsing with the surrender of Astoria to their Canadian rivals during the war
of 1812.

Furs were always valuable, but the old beaver
hat, which every well-dressed gentleman,
whether in Europe or in our eastern cities then
must wear to be in the mode, brought a boom in
that animal's fur, for it was used as a staple in
making the felt for this hat. In London, the
chief fur trading center of the world, wholesale
beaver fetched as high as fifty shillings ($12.50)
a pound. If you like looking for the wheels in
life that turn other wheels, think of this: it was
the London dandy's high hat that made Jim
Bridger!

In this boom, western men—St. Louis was
then far west—Lisa and his associates, Ashley

and his partners and successors, had made small fortunes, and eastern financiers nothing. This was a situation, naturally, that could not last, for "money goes to money." Jim Bridger and his partners ought to have known that and given in, as they had to do eventually, for these rivals had, as the saying goes, money to burn. They were to build trading centers and kill the mountain rendezvous.

Right now they were here with huge supplies, a great number of men, and willing to offer better terms for others who would enlist with them. The free-trapper they could get with a better offer, but that worthy was no use as a pilot to the best trapping grounds. The systematic knowledge of the whole vast area, the streams that were flush and those that were depleted of beaver, was only in the head of the partners of the Rocky Mountain Fur Company. Vanderburgh and Drips who were in charge of the new company —the American Fur Company—proposed to remedy this defect by simply following Bridger and the others.

Not yet awhile, however. The Rocky Mountain leaders slipped out of the rendezvous and were gone, and their rivals were left looking at the crooked trail they left. They wintered among the Nez Perce and Flatheads, and again

ran away from their rivals for the spring hunt.
But Vanderburgh and Drips made up in determination what they lacked in experience.
Learning through the whispering of the leaves
that the Rocky Mountain company had planned
to hold the rendezvous at Pierre's Hole, they appeared there bright and early to greet the Rocky
Mountain men.

The summer of 1832, and it is marked mem-
orably by the coming of Bonneville—Benja-
min Bonneville, then a captain and later to become a Brigadier-General.  Bonneville was in
the mountains on a mixed commission: to learn
something of the country, the warlike disposi-
tions of the Indians, and to make a little money
in furs for the New York gentlemen who had
underwritten his excursion.  One is torn between
the charm that Washington Irving was able to
give his story of the adventures of this gentleman, and the loss of the captain's actual observations, which he had painstakingly prepared.
Irving made a story from these journals and
spiced it with more than a grain of imagination.
In any case it is on Irving that we must depend
largely for what happened in the rivalry.

A race had developed between the supply
trains of the rival companies.  Fitzpatrick took
word down to Bill Sublette to push forward as

quickly as possible. He left Sublette to bring back word to the trappers, and ran into a roving band of Blackfeet. They led him such a harrowing chase in the Black Hills that his hair turned white. He finally evaded them and came in behind Sublette, who had outfooted Fontenelle in charge of the rival train. But Captain Vanderburgh, a West Point graduate, was now determined. Fitzpatrick and Bridger had made an offer to him that they divide up the territory, but this he rejected. He must not be blamed too much for this, for Bridger and Fitzpatrick by now knew the whole country as no others did, and the American Fur Company's leaders knew so little that they were hardly in a position to make a bargain.

Meeting his supply train, Vanderburgh got what he wanted and pushed on along the trail Bridger and Fitzpatrick had taken. Irving says that the latter deliberately led Vanderburgh into the Blackfoot country. That is quite possible, but it should be remembered that Bridger and Fitzpatrick had been trapping it two seasons before. Here Vanderburgh, on his men reporting a Blackfoot encampment, made light of it, and taking a few men went to see for himself. He was contemptuous of the concern his men felt. He followed the trail into a ravine, and entered it without any hesitation and taking no precautions.  It was an ambush.  A bullet brought him down, one or two of his men who followed him were killed, while the rest escaped.

The sequel to this incident as Irving writes it has a nice touch of imagination.  He says, with a flourish, that in the meantime Fitzpatrick and Bridger in their eagerness to mislead Vanderburgh had "betrayed themselves into danger and got into a region infested by Blackfeet."  They had strutted through this very region like gamecocks the year previous!

Coming up with a party of Blackfeet, Irving continues, they watched each other warily.  The Blackfeet made friendly signs, and a little group from each party advanced to meet each other, and fraternized.  Jim Bridger now came riding up, his rifle across the pommel of his saddle.  Continuing in Irving's words: "From some unfortunate feeling of distrust, Bridger cocked his rifle just as the chief was extending his hand in friendship.  The quick ear of the savage caught the click of the lock, in a twinkling, he grasped the barrel, and the contents were discharged into the earth at his feet."

This picture of Jim Bridger allowing his trappers to fraternize with the Blackfeet, then approaching them and acting like a nervous ten-

derfoot is amusing. Fortunately a trapper who
served in the command has a few words to say
regarding the incident which gives us a much
better picture of what happened.

The Blackfoot chief made a sign of peace and
advanced into the open. Bridger went out to
meet him, taking only a Blackfoot girl married
to one of his trappers, to act as interpreter. When
close to the Indian he saw what he considered a
suspicious movement. It was not Bridger's way
to be uncertain in what he did. The hammer of
his rifle came back in earnest. He threw up his
rifle and fired, but the Indian was too quick for
him. The barrel was struck downward, the bullet plunging into the ground. The Indian tried
to wrest the gun from Bridger's hands. During
the struggle two arrows struck Bridger in the
back, and the Blackfoot, getting possession of
the rifle, felled Bridger with a blow, jumped
Bridger's horse and carried away the Blackfoot
girl.

Irving seems to think that Bridger's movement was treacherous, but the circumstances
point to Bridger's suspicions having been justi-
fied. How did it happen that Bridger was hit by
a couple of arrows and that the Indian chief was
not brought down by the much more accurate
fire of trappers' rifles? It is possible that what

Bridger actually detected was a sign from the Indian to a couple of concealed bowmen. By now Bridger's scalp was the greatest trophy in the mountains, and any ruse by which it might be taken would have brought fame to the successful warrior.

How tough Jim Bridger had grown by this time can well be imagined. One arrowhead was cut out, but the other was too deeply embedded and could not be extracted, yet he continued on the fall hunt and went with his party into its winter encampment. There were no doctors to treat wounds or illness, but the trappers developed practices for caring for themselves. The notched arrowhead used by the Indians was difficult to pull out, but using their sharp knives somebody usually "butchered" it out, and dressed the wound, clean beaver fur being placed over it before it was bandaged with strips of cloth or skin.

At this winter encampment Bridger's command had some visitors. They were a small band of trappers, and among them was a sandy-haired, blue-eyed youngster, twenty-two years of age, called Kit Carson. To make the occasion memorable, twenty raiding Blackfeet, slipped into the camp, and stole some horses, among them Bridger's racer, Grohean. Bridger called for thirty volunteers—Kit Carson was one of them, of course—and took the trail. These Blackfeet were astute. To delay the pursuit, while the horses were sent on ahead with a few men, the rest took up a nice position, which they hoped would lead to a few scalps to add to the trophy of the horses. Bridger was not to be caught by such tricks, however. He detected the Blackfoot trap, and advanced on it cautiously, making use of every bit of cover. Two Blackfoot warriors were lost before nightfall brought them a respite, and a chance to slip out of the engagement that had turned out to be a little tougher than they had anticipated.

The delay, however, had served the Blackfoot purpose. There was no chance of overtaking the horses now, and the chase was given up. The casualties in the trappers' ranks had been one man wounded—Kit Carson. It was the only wound he was to receive in his long career of adventure.

## CHAPTER VIII

### 'WARE THE BLANKET CHIEF!

THE brigades commanded by Bridger and Fitzpatrick (Milton Sublette had been forced to return to St. Louis with an injury to his leg, which had to be amputated. He died three years later at Fort Laramie) could out-trap their rivals, but the competition was beginning to tell. The Rocky Mountain Company was now out of the Indian trade, and paying for their supplies at mountain prices, which were four or five hundred per cent above their cost. Both supplies and Indian trade had been sources of profit to the previous owners. The American Fur Company was pushing their in-

fluence among the Indians. They had rebuilt
Henry's old fort at the junction of the Yellowstone and the Missouri, and set up another on
the former river. Bill Sublette and Robert
Campbell began to build Fort Laramie, known
first after Sublette as Fort William, and to use
it as a trading center.

We have a remarkable testimony about this
time, coming to us in a most indirect way, of the
respect, if not terror, Bridger's name inspired
among the Indians. In the spring following
Kit Carson's visit, Bridger took his trappers into
Colorado, where he was to have a run-in with
his old friends, the Arikaras. At the summer
rendezvous the rival trapping companies camped
side by side, without the slightest ill feeling,
good evidence that the American Fur Company
did not hold Bridger and Fitzpatrick responsible
for Vanderburgh's death.

Here Bridger and Fitzpatrick separated, the
latter going into the Crow country, taking with
him a titled Englishman, Capt. Sir William
Drummond Stewart, who was having an adventurous holiday in the mountains. The Crows
took Fitzpatrick off his guard, and stripped him
clean of his horses, equipment and furs. One
of the trappers who made a record of the incident, reports the speech made by the white

spokesman, when Fitzpatrick and Stewart protested against the robbery to the Crow Indian chief, as follows:

"It is true that you have sustained heavy losses. But that is not the fault of the Blanket Chief (Bridger). If your young men have been killed they were killed when attempting to rob or kill our captain's men. . . .

"It is true that you have many widows and orphans to support and that is bad. I pity the orphans and will help you to support them, if you will restore to my captain (Fitzpatrick) the property stolen from his camp. Otherwise the Blanket Chief will bring more horses and plenty of ammunition, and there will be more widows and orphans among the Crows than ever before."

The speech had its effect for Fitzpatrick's horses, equipment and furs were returned to him, and he hurried out of the Crow country.

That Bridger's reputation among the Indians should, at this stage, so far transcend that of so celebrated a leader and fighter as Fitzpatrick is noteworthy.

Elsewhere, too, we find this reference to Bridger's name as a means of escape. A small party of trappers was captured and stripped by the Indians. Then learning that the men belonged to Bridger's command they hastened to return everything they had taken. "What shall I tell the Blanket Chief?" one of the trappers asked. The Indians were lavish in their protests of good will.

When the leaders brought their men into the summer rendezvous that year (1834), their four years were up. Each of them had probably made a little money, but not the fortunes that had gone to the others. Streams were being depleted, the competition grown keen. No young leaders were coming up, whose turn it would be to take over the Rocky Mountain Fur Company, and the rivals in the field now made it an entirely different proposition. So the Rocky Mountain Fur Company was dissolved. Fitzpatrick, M. Sublette and Bridger formed a company, buying out Fraeb and Gervais. The former received for his interest forty horses, forty traps, eight guns and merchandise worth about a thousand dollars; the latter twenty horses, thirty traps, and five hundred dollars' worth of merchandise.

That fall Bridger again took his trappers, among them Kit Carson, into the Blackfoot country. The next year he and Fitzpatrick bought Fort Laramie. Dr. Marcus Whitman, the Oregon missionary, was a visitor at the summer rendezvous (1835), and Bridger, lighter by one arrowhead, guided the party on its way to the west as far as the Three Tetons. That year —between rendezvous and rendezvous—was enlivened by some encounters with Indians, three of which had some novel features that make them worth recounting.

The first of these was with a Crow chief called The Bold. With a considerable party The Bold picked up one of Bridger's trappers named Joe Meek, who in later years was to become a well-known citizen of the new Oregon. The Indian questioned Meek about his command, and Meek adroitly led him to believe that it was a small party. The chief sensing an easy way to make a killing, thereupon threatened Meek and forced him to guide the Indians to the encampment, which was just what the trapper wanted him to do.

The chief was flabbergasted when, looking down from a hill, he saw the size of the encampment, but already Bridger's scouts had spread the alarm of the approach of the band, and Bridger was coming out to them, mounted on a large white horse, conspicuous as life, and seemingly unattended. Bridger and his men were by now both wary and skilled. Half a dozen men had already passed up a ravine ahead of him; a hundred others had advanced behind him in concealment.

Bridger, when within speaking distance, shouted to Meek to ask The Bold to send a sub-chief to him so that they might talk, and a second chief called Little Gun was sent forward. Stripped clean, the approved ambassadorial costume, Bridger and Little Gun advanced to meet each other. When they came together, as if by magic the advance party and the line of riflemen showed themselves, with Little Gun within its circle.

Bridger then calmly suggested that an exchange of Meek for Little Gun be made, and The Bold consented, saying to Meek "he could not afford to give a chief for one white dog's scalp." That The Bold regarded Bridger's action in the light of good, Indian-like strategy is shown by the fact that a few months later he made a three-months' peace with Bridger, which both respected.

The second novel incident of Indian encounters in this period shows the Delaware's idea of breaking the monotony of the winter encampment. Bridger had a few of these Indians, skillful hunters, in his brigade. For a little excitement they took a couple of horses, and staked them outside the encampment. Horse was a bait that no Indian could resist. The scouts of a large Blackfoot party attempted to run them off, were shot for their pains and scalped by the Delawares. This resulted in what Bridger used to call a "squall." The whole band, whose number is given as eleven hundred, set out to avenge their scouts, but they found Bridger's camp not to be taken either by assault or by surprise. Advancing as near as they dared, they threw up a fortification of their own. For a couple of days the camps dared each other, neither side being damaged to any extent, until the Indians, tiring of the game, withdrew.

The third incident concerns those Bannocks, who seem to have had so little luck with Bridger. The Nez Perces, camping by the trappers, stole some horses from the Bannocks. The Pierced Noses were not a warlike crowd and feeling sure, evidently, that in a short while the heavy hand of the Bannocks would descend on them, they took a fine horse from their booty and made a present of it to Bridger. Bridger was holding the spirited animal by a lasso and standing at the entrance to his lodge or tipi, when, with a yell, the Bannocks broke into the encampment. Most of them, learning that it was Bridger's command they were invading, began to calm down, but not their chief, highly wroth at losing a horse he so greatly prized. Seeing Bridger holding that very horse, without any hesitation he ran up to the trapper leader, and jerked the lasso out of his hand. That any Indian should treat their celebrated captain with such disrespect was an insult not to be borne, and he was immediately shot down, and in a moment trappers were jumping on their horses, and the Bannock running for their lives. They were pursued relentlessly, and handled so severely when they took refuge on an island that the tribe was depleted of nearly all their fighting men.

The summer of 1836. It marks the coming of the first white women to the mountains, and the end of the last vestige of Ashley's Rocky Mountain Fur Company. Fitzpatrick bringing in the summer supplies, which he left at Fort Laramie, continued on as escort to Mrs. Whitman and Mrs. Spalding, traveling to Oregon to join their missionary husbands. They made the journey in a light two horse wagon, with a heavier one drawn by four horses for freight.

The white women were the sensation of the summer rendezvous, for the mountain Indians had never seen a white woman. To them, people of the outdoors, with faces and bodies burned in the sun and chapped in the cold, the soft pink and white skin of these ladies was almost a miracle.

Here the firm of Fitzpatrick, Sublette and Bridger was broken up. Milt had been out of the mountains for some time and was at the moment waiting his end at Fort Laramie. Fitzpatrick had for the last few years been handling the supply train, and was ready to drop out. The streams had been trapped steadily now for thirteen years, and there were four or five times as many men working them systematically. But Bridger's home was in the mountains, and when the American Fur Company took over their interests, he remained with the new company, heading its trapping parties in the mountains in association with Lucien Fontenelle, while Drips, who had been with Vanderburgh, took over the supplies.

There was no change whatever in Bridger's routine. The fall and spring hunt, the winter encampment and the summer rendezvous. Taking his trappers east, west, north and south, invading the Blackfoot country from time to time, and fighting them. Once we find him using a new means of pushing an attack on an island encampment of Blackfoot warriors. Getting his men to make little forts of sticks and bushes, he advanced them crawling, pushing these barricades before them over the open ground, and firing into the Blackfoot camp, killing thirty of them and wounding many others.

Once while encamped on some rocky ground, the Blackfeet in the crags shouted their defiance and challenge, after the Indian fashion. One of Bridger's Iroquois hunters was not willing to take such a taunt lying down. Pepping himself up with his tribal war dance, and shouting the old battle-cry that was first heard in colonial times, he made for the rocks with a number of game trappers at his heels. Bridger's men had grown so adroit by now, that an advantage in position meant little to them. Making use of every bit of cover, they were able to give the Blackfeet a little more than the fight they had asked for, the Iroquois returning to the encampment quite a hero.

The lean years were coming. The last summer rendezvous was held in 1839, the year that Jim Bridger returned after another visit to St. Louis. Much had happened in the ten years since Bridger had last gone home to St. Louis. The town itself had grown. Steamers were making regular trips on the Missouri, and the banks of that river were beginning to be dotted with settlements, home-makers staking out farms where in other days the buffalo had roamed.

He was only thirty-five, but a weather-beaten old mountain man, alert to the sense of everything that was happening around him. It was impossible for him to miss the undercurrent of restlessness among the Indians of the plains, nor did he fail to see the star of the Sioux rising like a bad omen in the skies. A youngster named Jim Baker, who was also to become famous as a scout and guide in later years, accompanied Bridger back on his return journey to the mountains. Speaking of the Indians thick on the plains and their menacing temper Baker says: "But thanks be to James Bridger for our safety, because I learned then and later of his great knowledge of, and ability to treat with, the redskins, which was never excelled by any scout of the plains."

As if to celebrate the last opportunity before the end of the epoch that he saw coming, Bridger made some long journeys with small groups—always trapping—the details of which have been completely lost: following the Colorado south, the Gila across Arizona and New Mexico, through the province of Chihuahua to the Gulf; through California and Oregon into Canada.

Bridger could see the shadow of coming events. In 1841 the Sioux and Cheyennes had

attacked Fraeb and killed him and four others.
Bridger, taking a fur train to St. Louis the next
year, fell in with a party belonging to John C.
Fremont, bound for the mountains to survey the
route through the South Pass. Bridger gave
them information of the warlike temper of the
Sioux, and offered to help them out. He met
also a band of emigrants, who were fortunate
enough to secure the services of no less a person
than old Fitzpatrick to guide them. A few
weeks on the plains had turned them into a
mighty discouraged number of individuals. At
Fort Laramie some of them had lost faith in the
promise of Oregon, selling their cattle, even
their clothes.

Bridger's mind must have been already made
up, for when he returned in the spring of 1843,
it was with supplies for a fort he was to build in
partnership with Louis Vasquez, who had been
a trapping companion of many years, Vasquez
having been present with the party on Bear
River when young Jim Bridger set out on that
journey in the bull-boat nearly twenty years before that had led to the waters of Great Salt
Lake.

Choosing a point along the great trail on the
further side of South Pass, where the Green
River broke into a number of forks, a great val-

ley in which grass was plentiful and luxuriant, with trees lining sparkling streams full of trout, Bridger and Vasquez set up the "fort." It was a mean enough structure of mud and sticks, nothing more than a trading post, but it had a little blacksmith's shop and a carpenter's shop, where necessary repairs could be made. It was set up for the "convenience of emigrants," and those conveniences should be measured in terms of the wilderness. It was many weeks' journey from Fort Laramie, and there was nothing beyond it until the western settlements were reached. It must not be supposed that the two owners stayed around their fort all the year round. Wandering was too much in their blood. It was a summer trading center, and even in that period it was sometimes deserted, especially in the early years.

Bridger had by his fortuitous discovery of the South Pass twenty years earlier, found the key to the conquest of the mountains; now his fort was to mark a new period in our development. Henry M. Chittenden says: "The return of Lewis and Clark, and the founding of Fort Bridger determine the limits of a distinct period in western history."

# PART III

## TRAIL-BREAKER

## CHAPTER IX

### "Oh, Susannah"

JIM BRIDGER was what the mountain men called a "Great Leg," that is, a man whose endurance was so great and whose pace was so swift that few could keep up with him. At a pinch, on foot, these men could easily make a hundred miles a day. Long journeys Bridger had made during his trapping days, and continued to make during the fall, winter and spring for many years after his fort was established. When on exploration bent his journeys were with one or two men, often Indians, but frequently alone. On one of these long trips he did not see a white man for eighteen months. Many of these journeys were conducted on foot, probably using snow shoes. On one occasion it is said that he followed the Mackenzie River to the Arctic Ocean.

His knowledge of the far west stretched from the frozen plains of the north to the sub-tropical plains of Mexico, and it was a knowledge that no single man could duplicate. Bridger had tramped and ridden a vast territory in search of beaver in the course of twenty years. He saw in pictures like an artist, and could draw these pictures with fascinating skill. He was enamored of the mountains, entranced by their natural wonders, and was led to pry constantly into every secret they held.

To-day a chain of national parks marks the wonders of the Rockies for us, from Glacier to Mesa Verde and the Indian Trail, and provides the most unique collection of natural phenomena of any mountain range in the world. The tourists who visit these parks in their thousands, and are forewarned by guide-books of everything they will see, gasp at the eerie charm of the Grand Canyon and the Mesa Verde, and cannot avoid a little nervousness in the Yellowstone's exhibit of fire and brimstone and spouting geyser. Long after Bridger made it his home, the people of the United States regarded these mountains with

THE RENDEZVOUS

only a mild and indifferent interest. Cultured eastern gentlemen when they found need to mention them in their writings referred to them as the "American Alps." They held Bridger, however, as with a spell. He constantly returned to examine their natural wonders, listened to Indian legends concerning them, and tried to find an explanation of their phenomena.

All this had combined in making his mind a vast storehouse of knowledge of the far west, and when he found himself suddenly engulfed in a wave of humanity moving across his wilderness, that knowledge became of priceless value, though truth to tell that wave of humanity at first was not interested in his mountains, merely in getting over them to the promised land of Oregon and California.

There were, of course, two different and distinct movements. The first was the march of the land-hungry who wanted a home with plenty of elbow room in the fertile wilderness. It was a movement of moderate proportions as to numbers. A large number of the people whom we have noticed in the first trains of 1841, 1842, and 1843 were backwoodsmen. We can almost measure the flow of the Oregon tide by the numbers: nine hundred men, women and children who set out from Independence, Mo., in 1843 to fourteen hundred the next year, and three thousand the year following. It was a movement that was not so important for its numbers as for its effect in winning for the American nation the territories that now comprise the states of Washington, Oregon and Idaho.

The history of Oregon goes back to the sixteenth century when Spanish mariners first discovered it. Francis Drake, nosing along this coast in the *Golden Hind,* pilfering the Spanish galleons and looking for the northwest passage, had taken possession of it in the name of his queen and called it Albion. Capt. Cook had explored parts of it. The accidental discovery that furs, bartered from the Indians, could be traded in China at a good profit for tea and silk had led, during the eighteenth century to some interest in the territory on the part of both British and American merchant seamen. One of these, Capt. Gray, had in 1792 found the river of the west, and named it after his ship, the *Columbia.*

President Jefferson had early realized the value of Oregon, and the need of exploring it by land, and finally persuaded Congress to allot two thousand five hundred dollars for a "literary pursuit," the Lewis and Clark expedition. Astor's land and water party, which had estab-

lished Astoria and some other trading centers,
sold them during the war of 1812 to the British.

The Treaty of Ghent, which terminated that
war, agreed that both sides should return everything they had captured. On Gray's discoveries
and these facts the American claim to these territories rested. Spain and Russia put forward
some claims to this country too, but the former
resigned hers when she sold Florida to the
United States, and an agreement was made with
Russia that settled her Alaskan boundary. England not only continued her claim, but her interests through the Hudson Bay Company, which
absorbed the Northwest Fur Company, were
dominant in the territory during Bridger's early
days in the mountains.

In 1818 England and America agreed to a
joint occupation, and in 1827 renewed it for an
indefinite period, on the understanding that the
agreement could be voided by either party on
twelve months' notice. Nobody wanted the
country particularly, except the fur-traders, who
at that time found plenty of elbow room for their
trapping parties, their rivalry turning on buying
rival trappers with better offers, or making a
purchase of furs from Indians or free-trappers
who were under the influence of the other party.

Interest in the country among people in the

east developed through a rather curious incident.
In 1832 two old Salish Indian chiefs, with an
escort of younger braves, made a journey from
their Oregon hunting grounds to St. Louis to
ask for a copy of the Great Medicine Book of
the Whites (the Bible) and a Black Robe (missionary) who would explain it to them. Lewis
and Clark had met these Indians on their famous
journey, and it was to "Red Head," William
Clark, now Indian agent at St. Louis, that they
brought their plea. That they took this request
to Clark rather than to their neighbors, the Hudson Bay Company, or even the Rocky Mountain
trappers, suggests that it might have been something Clark had said to them or his personality
that had sent them on such a hazardous journey,
for it crossed the country of many hostile tribes.
Clark could not, of course, supply them with a
missionary. The two old chiefs died in St.
Louis; the young braves returned to their tribe
empty-handed.

Naturally enough the incident attracted attention. Here were primitive seekers for truth
among our own savages, and the romantic
glamor of their appeal spoke swiftly to our
churches, which had been for many years sending missionaries to foreign countries. Jason and
Daniel Lee of the Methodist Mission went out

in 1834 by boat, and we have already noted Dr. Marcus Whitman's journey the year following. Two or three years later the Roman Catholics established a mission station in the Oregon country.

The attention called to this country through these incidents resulted not only in the emigrants setting out for that land, but to a political agitation that came to a head in 1844 when the Democratic Convention made the retaining of Oregon a plank in their platform, and their slogan "54.40 or Fight" (54 degrees 40 minutes North latitude as boundary) the keynote of their campaign. The Democratic candidate, James K. Polk, was elected. Negotiations were already, however, under way, and in the year following President Polk taking office, a treaty was signed with Great Britain establishing the Oregon country as an American possession with the boundary along the 49th parallel, but by this time the American population in Oregon had grown to about ten thousand and was actually dominant in the country.

The California emigrant who crossed Jim Bridger's mountains differed greatly from the Oregon settler. California was Mexican territory, settled and jealously held by a long line of missions and ranches. Spanish California had

a life, if not a civilization all its own. The
people led an easy, picturesque, carefree existence, providing a sharp contrast to the eager,
forceful and hardworking American frontier
settler. As noted in the Jedediah Smith incident, they frowned on immigration, but it was
almost impossible to keep the American out.

Some of the Oregon emigrants had turned
south to settle in northern California. Many
trappers had found their way into the country.
In 1841 a party entered Southern California by
the Santa Fe trail, and later parties entered the
country by the Oregon trail, turning south at
Fort Hall, and making their way through the
hard desert country into California itself. The
Mexicans looked on these inroads with alarm,
for California was only thinly populated, and
where Americans in any number were settled
they had shown a tendency to form a government
of their own.

John C. Fremont on his third surveying journey for the government came into the country
in 1845, and finding the settlers alarmed at a
decree that called on them either to be natural-
ized or deported, took part in the Bear Flag
Revolution, which was short lived, for hardly
had the protests of the Mexican Government
been made than the United States had formally

declared war with Mexico over causes that had nothing to do with this situation. The naval forces took Monterey immediately, and the whole country fell into American hands without a single battle of any importance. The heaviest casualties suffered were in the fight at San Pascual in which Kit Carson took part, when sixteen were killed and nineteen badly wounded. Fremont's part in the events connected with the California conquest led to his being court-martialed, and on his being found guilty of mutiny, disobedience, and misconduct, to his resigning from the service. Long before the country passed into American hands, through the treaty of Guadalupe Hidalgo of 1848, a steady flow of emigrants had set in.

The Oregon and California land emigrants had been merely a ripple in the pool of our national life—Oregon was mental excitement rather than physical movement—and probably the sentiment of the majority of northern settlers was one of regret, for there was almost no market for their cattle, or the wheat and fruit they grew. The nation, too, was in a blue mood, wrapt in the pessimism of a post-war deflation period, when suddenly the magic word, "Gold," swept not merely the whole country, but the whole world.   The interest jumped in a few months to a fever.

John Marshall, a foreman at Sutter's Fort, while building a sawmill, made the discovery of gold in California, though he was destined to get little benefit out of it.   The find was made in January 1848.   There had been talk of gold in California for a number of years, and when the first word of Marshall's discovery spread about there was little interest.   But once it was realized that here at last was the real thing, practically every American in California took his pick and shovel and set off for the hills. Soldiers deserted; sailors "jumped" their ships; workshops were left without a man; small towns were sometimes completely deserted.

News took a long time to travel in that day. California was then more isolated from New York than the interior of Africa is from us to-day.   There was no regular communication by land, and sailing ships had to round the Horn between Atlantic and Pacific ports or sail around the world, an absence of three years being an ordinary occurrence for a trading vessel which might set out from Boston with a cargo for California or Oregon, picking up merchandise there which it could exchange in the Orient for tea, silk and spices, and making the run back to its

home port round the Cape of Good Hope. Incidentally, it was the needs of quicker communication with California that stretched the
famous clipper ships to making their record-
breaking runs.

Whatever doubts the East might have had as
to the discovery were quickly dispelled when the
Governor of California reported that there was
gold enough in the mountains to pay the cost of
the war with Mexico a hundred times over.

It was the tonic east and west needed—the
east blue from the post-war depression; Oregon
settlers with good grain, fruit and meat they
could not sell. Those who remained in that
country now found that a golden age had dawned
for them. They could sell their wheat in a
California port for five dollars a bushel; butter
at one dollar and twenty-five cents a pound;
apples at anything up to a dollar apiece; beef
twenty-five cents a pound on the hoof. In the
east talk of going to the gold fields was the only
topic of conversation. Europe caught the infec-
tion. Men were jumping off even from Aus-
tralia for the promised land. And well they
might, for gold was to be had almost for the
taking, and stories both true and exaggerated
that came of wealth picked up in a few days, of
the careless indifference with which the miners

spent these gains, served only to inflame imaginations already glowing with pictures of the new El Dorado. Clubs were formed in our eastern cities. France had lotteries in which the lucky winners were given a trip to California. "Susannah" was the popular song of the day:

> "Oh, Susannah, don't you cry for me,
>   I'm off to California with my wash bowl on my knee."

The journey was no easy undertaking, however. By sea it meant rounding the Horn, or crossing the Isthmus of Panama and again taking a boat. In either case the journey was long, arduous, and expensive. The Panama journey in the matter of speed had an advantage over both the overland and the Cape Horn routes, and was consequently the most popular. The rush by that route started as early as the Fall of 1848.

It was too late then to start the journey across the continent, but that winter was a period of preparation. Parties began to flow towards the Missouri and converge at points where the plains journey would begin. Excitement there was, and rivalry, too, for men were anxious to beat each other to the wealth that lay on the other side of the great mountains. That spring—the spring of 1849—no less than thirty thousand people were waiting at Independence, Mo., to follow the great trail, and forming a line of wagons so long, that the Indians looking down on that endless procession were astounded that any tribe could be so large.

# CHAPTER X

## OREGON ROAD

THE Great Medicine Road of the Whites that the forty-niners traversed was as clearly marked then as any transcontinental boulevard to-day. Parts of it had been a game trail, which generations of Indians had followed in their wanderings. Nearly all of it was marked by the trappers within four or five years after Bridger's discovery of the South Pass, Hugh Glass's journey down the Platte by bull-boat, and Ashley's mule and horse train with supplies. Long before the first emigrant wheel turned on it there were dozens of men who not only had traversed it, but could tell

every problem that would be encountered along
the long trail, and how best to meet it—the rivers
and their favored crossings; where grass would
be found in abundance and where it would be
found lacking; where wood was plentiful and
the miles in which not a stick would be found;
the various tribes of Indians through whose
hunting grounds it passed, and how best to treat
with them.

Names had grown around every landmark,
most of them bound in adventures of twenty
years of trappers' history: Independence Rock
after a party that had camped there on July 4th
and celebrated in the robust fashion of that day;
Laramie after a man who had lost his life there;
Crazy Woman where a voyageur's wife had
gone out of her mind; the Sweetwater because
of its contrast with the muddy water of the
Platte; Scott's Bluff, where a man of that name
had lost his life. One version of that story was
that the canoe in which Scott and his party was
traveling had overturned. All the weapons and
foodstuff they carried was lost. They tried to
make their way back on foot, living on roots and
berries, and soon found themselves exhausted
and starved. In this condition Scott had fallen
ill and could not keep up with the party. He
was left behind when fresh sign of the trail of

some white men was found, and the stronger
members of the party pushed ahead to find help.
When they eventually got back Scott was found
dead, having dragged himself a long distance
after the others. Some story or incident marked
every important point on the trail for the
trappers.

These men, of course, had no grand idea of
naming places for posterity. The names clung
to the places simply by the constant reference
to the incident when any one wanted to refer to
a certain place. Thus the valley in which Pierre
the Iroquois hunter was ambushed by the Blackfeet became Pierre's Hole; Jackson's Hole the
place where Bridger found him when the rest
of the parties lost touch with that leader. South
Pass was called the Southern Pass merely to distinguish it from the ones farther north where
Henry's men had crossed the divide. Cache
Valley took that name because here the trappers
had one season hidden much of their furs. The
French word *cache* was the regular term these
men employed for storing furs or extra supplies
and equipment. A hole was dug in the ground
or an excavation made in an embankment, and
lined with sticks and leaves to prevent dampness
getting to the stores. Every handful of earth
was carefully disposed of, the original clods of

earth replaced on the top. Indians made a constant practice of stealing these caches, and wolves and other animals would dig into them if the human scent was not removed. To prevent the latter the top was usually watered to remove human odor. To circumvent the Indians the whole place had to be left without any trace of what had been done; yet its position between trees, bowlders or some prominent object must be so clearly marked that one party could describe it to another.

Other places took their name from some natural phenomena or resemblance, like Bridger's Two Ocean Pass, Stinking River, Three Forks, Chimney Rock, Powder River, Soda Springs, Salt Lake. Thus unconsciously the entire trail, and much of the world of the trapper, was named and laid out for the newcomers who were to make a new page in its history.

As to wheels that were now to turn along the great trail in endless line, Sublette had rolled Ashley's cannon along in 1826, and brought his supplies in by wagon train in 1830. Booneville took a wagon train through the Pass two years later, and in 1836 Fitzpatrick had escorted the missionary ladies to the mountain rendezvous, whence others had taken them along into Oregon.

We think of the covered wagon trail to-day as a glamorous adventure, an orderly progression, with hardships met with grim determination, with charging Indians shattered by telling fire from a circular corral, with dashing heroes riding spirited horses, an epic of the happy-go-lucky, never-say-die spirit. There are glimpses of it, of dancing to fiddles, of youngsters falling in love with each other, the hardships merely something that gave an added pique to a great adventure.

On the whole, despite the years of traveling on the trail done by trappers, the emigrants suffered incredible hardships. From these thousands perished as they toiled along the trail; other thousands died of disease and accidents; many lost their lives to Indians; some even committed suicide. The difference between ease and suffering seems to have lain in good captains and the services of an able guide. The captain in charge depended on the willingness of the train to place authority in the hands of one man, and the choice of that man for his ability—not an easy thing always to find and decide on. A thoroughly competent guide was expensive, even when a mountain man could be induced to pilot the train. There was much bigger work than piloting single trains for men of the caliber of

Bridger and Fitzpatrick, even if the trains could afford to pay for their services. "Broken Hand" Fitzpatrick took the first trains through with ease, where later ones toiled and suffered.

If the discouragements of the trail were suffered by the tenderfeet, who came in an increasing stream after forty-nine, one can better understand some of the somber pictures of that day, but the emigrants we have noticed in a preceding chapter who sold their cattle and clothes at Laramie were backwoodsmen making their way to the new country, the best equipped of any group of our citizens to make the long journey.

Francis Parkman, the historian, who spent a summer on the Oregon Trail in 1847 (two years before the great wave), found the trains with hardy settlers from the border states, seething with dissension, and almost completely at sea. "On visiting the encampment we were at once struck with the extraordinary perplexity and indecision that prevailed among them." The men glum, "the women were divided between regret for the home they had left and fear of the deserts and savages before them." They let their wagons and stock straggle, and the latter were often run off by horse-lifting Indians. All along the trail were abandoned furniture, tables, bureaus

and other articles, family treasures some of them
inherited from colonial ancestors. In a few
years the entire trail was marked by things abandoned—from wagons to tools with which the
artisan hoped to set himself up in the new land.
Parkman tells of two men who went looking for
stray horses without a gun or a pistol between
them. To a couple of Pawnee braves this
seemed too good to be true, and an arrow was
promptly dispatched that brought one of the
white men down, while the other escaped. The
whole train was so terrified that they formed
camp and would not budge for several days, or
make any effort to recover the body of their
slain comrade. In a trade the emigrants Parkman met seemed so afraid that they would be
cheated that even after agreeing to an exchange,
they would change their minds about giving
something they did not want for something they
did. Their uncertainty when dealing with the
Indian was so marked that the Sioux were treat-
ing them with studied arrogance, pulling up
every train and demanding a feast from each.

Parkman felt himself unduly superior to the
emigrants. They were risking everything they
had, knowing only what lay in front of them by
hearsay, while he was taking a pleasure jaunt,
and had besides a seasoned and well-known

hunter to guide him—a man who could tell a
Kansas from a Sioux a half mile away, and knew
every woodlot and water-course on the trail.
Yet the fact remains that in this new world of
the endless prairie, even the hardy frontier settler was lost. It was endless. To him it was
without any landmark, and day after day nothing
appeared to relieve the monotony. The very
fact that they had lived their lives in a forested
country would add to this strangeness of feeling,
much as a landlubber might feel in a small boat
when there is no land in sight.

The first group of eastern tenderfeet to go
over this trail was a party of men recruited in
Boston and other eastern towns by Nathaniel J.
Wyeth, who aimed to establish a fur-trading and
salmon fishing business in the Oregon country.
His company consisted of a few adventurous
spirits and mechanics who could work at their
respective trades in the forts he planned to build.
His young cousin, John B. Wyeth, who with a
number of other men, deserted him before the
journey to Oregon was completed, and returned
to Boston, wrote a little book of his experiences.
Wyeth crossed the plains in 1832 in company
with Bill Sublette, and the only losses his company suffered were a blacksmith's forge and a
cask of powder, when Nathaniel Wyeth disre-

garding Sublette's advice that he float his stuff
across the Platte on bull-boats chose to follow
eastern practice and used a raft instead. Sublette would have described the whole journey as
being without incident; to young John Wyeth it
was an appalling experience, and his pathos to-
day seems a little humorous. To the New England youngster the necessity of using, during one
period of the journey, buffalo chips—dried dung
of the buffalo—for fuel in cooking, epitomized
the whole dreadful country. One can only
imagine how a little group of emigrants, cast on
their own resources might feel, as they traversed
this country day after day. Sudden thunder-
storms, furious rain squalls, everything empha-
sized a different world.

As the journey progressed the clear atmosphere of the uplands brought a puzzling difference to eyes trained in the different perspec-
tive of the eastern landscape. A mountain that
looked no more than five miles distant, turned
out to be forty or fifty miles away. At long
range it was impossible to tell the difference between a band of Indians and a herd of buffalo.
The mountain man from long experience told
them apart only by slight variations in color.
Even trained eyes would be deceived often.
Parkman tells of his guide, Henry Chatillon, a

well-known frontier character, who saw a black speck on a swell of the prairie, and pronounced it to be a grizzly bear. "So we all galloped forward together, prepared for a hard fight; for these bears, though clumsy in appearance, are incredibly fierce and active. The swell of the prairie concealed the black object from our view. Immediately after it appeared again. But now it seemed very near to us; and as we looked at it in astonishment, it suddenly separated into two parts, each of which took wing and flew away. We stopped our horses and looked at Henry, whose face exhibited a curious mixture of mirth and mortification. His eye had been so completely deceived by the peculiar atmosphere that he had mistaken two large crows at a distance of fifty rods (two hundred and seventy-five yards) for a grizzy bear a mile off." Imagine how the emigrant felt when he found his eyes playing a hundred tricks like this each day!

Game, and especially buffalo was plentiful. Indian and trapper took them with ease because their long experience had taught them many things. The emigrant could lose himself galloping after a herd. The soft bullet from his rifle unless placed just right only resulted in the animal taking a long run before he fell, if he was badly wounded.  It is surprising to read in the experiences of tenderfeet on the plains of long buffalo chases in which inexperienced men fired dozens of shots without succeeding in bringing down a single buffalo.

Almost every experience to the emigrant on the plains seemed menacing.  The muddy water while following the Platte, which gave him dysentery and other diseases; the necessity of fording swift streams; the woodless and waterless stretches; the lack of landmarks; even the very buffalo they might want for food.  What would happen when a herd of buffalo descended on them and engulfed the train?  It looked as if they would be crushed in the stampede.  The mountain men knew that if they corralled and guarded their stock to prevent straggling with the herd no danger was to be feared from the buffalo which would pass on either side of the corral, but even if the emigrant had been told this, consider the state of mind of the men caught in such an experience, until the danger was passed.

And the Indian.  He was restless, aggrieved, and saw in the movement of emigrants the beginning of the end of his game trails.  Men like Bridger had learned to deal with them through a lifetime of experience.  When one could not

tell a Kansas from a Crow, or a Pawnee from a
Sioux, there was little hope that he could do
any better when he was called upon to deal with
the varying temper of the tribesmen out on a
raiding party, hunting or simply moving camp.
Their swagger was disconcerting, and even their
friendly visits were often paid by a body of
horsemen riding like a cyclone, shouting and
yelling, discharging their muskets, and when the
impact seemed certain breaking like a wave
around the encampment. A horse carelessly
looked after was a sore temptation even to a
friendly Indian. The mountain men met them
all with a bold front and an unhasty hand on
the trigger, knowing that even if he was in small
numbers the Indians' refusal to take a loss of
even one man, gave him an advantage, for he was
never willing to swap a brave, let alone a chief,
for "one white dog's scalp." In a really serious
engagement the trappers on this trail had learned
to swing the front and rear of his supply or fur
train in a circle, and to build a barricade of his
packs, with his horses in the center. The emigrants did not learn such tactics for many years.
Their heavy wagons were ideally adapted for
such defense. It was through Bridger's influence that later emigrant trains were led to adopt

this effective protection both for the night corral
and as a means of defence in Indian attack.

The real trials of the California journey came
beyond Bridger's fort, when the trains, having
turned south from Fort Hall, followed the Bear
River into the desert country. It was here that
some of the most terrible tragedies of the gold
rush days took place. The plains and mountain
trail strewn with things discarded was nothing
as compared to the mute tokens that marked
every foot of the desert trail. Men and women,
horses and cattle perished here in great numbers.
There was little water and grass was scarce.
Disease took a heavy toll. Its natural hardships
were multiplied through the desire to make as
much speed as possible into the gold country.
Much of the early troubles of the emigrant began in the natural tendency of the tenderfoot to
weight himself down with as heavy a load as he
could carry.

Not all the thousands who went to California
and Oregon passed through Fort Bridger. Between South Pass and Fort Hall the trail took a
great bend, and it was along this elbow that
Bridger's fort was located. A more direct
route from South Pass—Sublette's cut-off—was
shorter by about one hundred and fifty miles.
The disadvantage of the short cut was that it

had no water or grass for more than fifty miles, but great numbers, eager to make speed, followed it.

A printed guide book for the use of those making the overland journey, pulished in the early fifties, contains in its advertising columns the following notice, evidently written by the man who prepared the book:

### FORT BRIDGER

Tired emigrants will find here a home where their wants will be supplied. It is an excellent resting place, as thousands of emigrants who have shared the hospitality of Col. Bridger, the commandant of the fort and owner of the trading post, have attested. Everything needed for variety or health can be obtained here.

Col. Bridger has lived here twenty-nine years; is well acquainted with the mountains, Indians, etc.; can and will furnish much valuable information to emigrants. His post is 131 miles beyond South Pass, 113 to Salt Lake City, 100 miles to Soda Springs, down the Bear River. Five miles beyond the springs, the road forks—the right hand goes to Fort Hall, and the left is the nighest and best road for California.

There are many references to Fort Bridger in the diaries and reminiscences of those who paused there while making the overland journey. It was improved somewhat in the course of the years, a description of it states that in 1849 it had a huge picket fence, and some chairs. Trade was excellent, many thousands encamping in the pleasant valley in which the Fort was built, resting their horses and cattle, the men and women recuperating in the pleasant shade, fishing the trout in the streams, and visiting with the Indians who were present there each summer. It was also a summer rendezvous for a few old trappers who still worked the streams, as Bridger continued to do when possible in the fall and spring months. As the emigrants increased in number a few other mountain men took up their abode in the valley, opened little trading posts and operated ferries over the branches of the Green River.

Jim Bridger guided no private trains and his dealings with the emigrants were entirely in trade, advice and help. Some years later he built a ferry at the Platte River crossing, using a flatboat that was propelled by the force of the current. This automatic device is still used in the crossing of swift streams in some parts of the world. The bow of the boat is fastened to a cable that stretches across the river and along which the boat can slide easily. To move it across the stream the steersman gets the boat into position with the nose pointing upstream at an angle. The current dashing against the sides of the boat drives it forward in much the same way as a sailing boat tacks into the wind.

Bridger's personality and fame made him a natural prey to the tenderfoot bent on idle questions, or asking for advice he was not willing to follow. When asked regarding any part of the long trail Bridger would carefully give from his vast knowledge, the best camping spots, points at which good pasture and water would be found. The tenderfoot would then refer to the guide book he had purchased at the Missouri crossing, sold in the thousands for a few cents a copy, and find that Bridger's advice differed from that in the book. The more inexperienced a man was the more prone he was to believe that everybody was trying to take advantage of him, and clearly if the advice did not agree with the book then he was being deceived! There was nothing particularly wrong with the guide-books, of course; but since thousands of people followed the same advice, the grass at the camping spots recommended would be eaten for miles around. Other questions, too, would be shot at him in an endless stream, and an army officer who knew him well says that he saw Bridger sometimes sitting under a tree pretending that he was deaf and dumb!

In contrast we have the record of many appreciations for his kindness, his hospitality and his help. One of these, made by William Kelly, a forty-niner, speaks of Bridger being "excessively kind and patient with me in laying down the route." He drew a map for Kelly with a piece of charcoal on the door of his trading post, showing him a route that would cut off thirty miles to Salt Lake City, which Kelly took. Bridger also lent Kelly the workshop, so that he could make some repairs to his wagon. This was a great deal, simply in money, for at Fort Laramie, some six hundred miles from the Missouri settlements, the blacksmith charged three dollars to put on a single horse-shoe; here, three times that distance in the wilderness, such rude conveniences as Bridger had were worth a great deal. Mrs. B. C. Ferris, journeying with her husband to Salt Lake City where he was to take up his duties as Secretary of the territory of Utah, and coming into Fort Bridger at the fall of the year, says: "This man (Bridger) strongly attracted my attention; there was more than civility about him—there was native politeness. He alarmed us in regard to our prospects of getting through; said the season had arrived when a heavy snow might be looked for any day; asked us to stay with him all winter; showed us where we could lodge, guarded against the cold with plenty of buffalo skins, and assured us that he could make the benefit of our society and the assistance of Mr. Ferris in his business more than compensate for the expense of living. This was a delicate way of offering the hospitality of his establishment without remuneration. He told us if we were to go to make as little delay as possible; and made a very acceptable addition to our larder in the shape of fresh potatoes and other vegetables." Others speak of Mrs. Bridger giving them milk and buttermilk, a luxury indeed in the wilderness.

Although the actual time Bridger spent in the fort was small, the business he established with Vasquez paid him well—if, indeed, it did not give him for a short while the illusion of feeling a rich man.

## CHAPTER XI

### Highway Marker

BRIDGER'S trading post is only an interlude in his story. Its pleasant location and its conveniences proved of great help to those who traveled the great trail. Once such trading became a great business, competition was again to run him out. Looking back we can feel even a little grateful that twice when it looked as if he might grow wealthy and perhaps retire to the humdrum life of the settlements things happened to keep him in his beloved mountains. Bridger Pass, Bridger Mountain, Bridger Creek, Bridger Peak, Bridger Crossing, Bridger Lake, were yet to be named after him; the other great new routes with which his fame is also linked, were yet to be laid out. The years of service that followed added greatly to his fame, and left its mark all over the mountain states, so that to-day the figure of the trapper who looks down from the capitols of both Montana and Colorado is in the likeness of Jim Bridger.

Such knowledge as Bridger possessed of the mountains became of value immediately the government decided, now that the whole west was American territory and vast numbers of people were moving across them, more accurate maps should be made, and other trails marked for the progressive development they saw ahead of it.

In 1849 Captain Howard Stansbury and Lt. John W. Gunnison, topographical engineers of the army, were ordered to make a survey of the Salt Lake Valley, and engaged Bridger to guide them. This was the first of a number of surveying parties which he piloted.

To both Stansbury and Gunnison, Bridger seemed the most remarkable find. He was a walking map. He told them of the mound builders in the south; of the mysterious Yellowstone in the north. He saw in pictures and his descriptions of places and scenes were vivid.

Gunnison compares his speech as equal in clarity and wealth of description to one of the most noted writers of the day. More than this they were surprised to find that Bridger was an artist. Even with such crude materials as a door and a piece of charcoal he left no doubt as to the details he wished to portray. Gunnison writes of this gift: "His graphic sketches are delightful romances. With a buffalo skin and a piece of charcoal he will map out any portion of this immense region and delineate mountains, streams and the circular valleys called 'holes' with wonderful accuracy; at least we may so speak of that portion we traversed *after* descriptions were given."

The following year he guided another exploring party to the Yellowstone River, and later that year Bridger took Stansbury, over a route he had discovered, and on which much of the romance of the west was later to be written. Stansbury says that Bridger undertook this "with great spirit," "although at a considerable sacrifice of his own interests."

The trail on which Bridger led Captain Stansbury followed the South Platte to Lodgepole to Cheyenne Pass to Bridger Pass to Bitter Creek, to the Green River and Black Fork, where it joined the Oregon Road near his own fort.

In this manner there came into history the famous Overland Trail over which those gallant youngsters were for a year to ride the eight-day Pony Express from St. Jo to the coast. Here, too, came the Stage Coach, bringing with it the dime-novel days of the hold-up man, and finally the rails of the Union Pacific, and all these changes Jim Bridger was to see come to pass. Both Pony Express and Overland Stage were to pull up at Fort Bridger on their regular run to change riders and horses.

There is a pretty story of the engineers of the Union Pacific, baffled by the failure to find a pass through the mountains, sending as a last resort for Jim Bridger to come to Denver and help them, of the old man walking into the drafting room and on being told what they wanted, laying a sheet of drafting paper on the floor, picking up a piece of charcoal from the fire, and drawing a map, pointing out a pass which would not only take them over, but which would need little grading. General Grenville M. Dodge, who knew Bridger well, and employed him as guide and scout in his Indian campaigns, and who joined the Union Pacific as its chief engineer after he resigned from the army, says this story isn't true; that Bridger was of great service to them, but not in quite that

dramatic way.  Bridger assisted him in the final
U. P. surveys.  An anecdote of Bridger's uncanny powers of observation deals with the preliminary survey of the railroad.  The man in
charge was running a trail line far north of the
route that was eventually decided on, when he
met Bridger.  Bridger told him that he would
find Lodgepole a much lower pass than those he
would encounter on the line he was taking, and
the surveyor checked up and found this to be
correct.  How could Bridger tell the height of
these passes?  He had no instruments.  He went
over them at different times, usually bent on
some business that had nothing to do with com-
paring the height of one place with another.

Bridger had worked out the railroad's problem in his own mind many years before there was
actual need for such knowledge or before he
was called upon to help the surveyors.  The
Union Pacific was opened to traffic in 1869.
Many years before that—to be exact, in 1853—
the editor of the Kansas City Journal inter-
viewed Bridger on one of his periodic journeys
to the "settlements."  On that occasion Bridger
drew for this editor "with a piece of charcoal on
a piece of wrapping paper an outline of the
route necessary to be taken by a railroad should
it ever cross the continent, which route is ex-

actly on the line that is now crossed by the Union Pacific."

In the following years the business rivalry that was to run him out of Fort Bridger came to a head. As the final result of this was to bring him the first assignment as a government scout, we have reserved its telling for another section. In 1854 passing down the plains in the fall, at Fort Laramie Bridger ran into a party the like of which the prairies had never seen. It was a one-man hunting party, bound for the mountains and the pleasures of the chase, but it consisted of six wagons and twenty-one carts, and a considerable retinue including two scientists. It was loaded down with every luxury imaginable, carried an arsenal of a variety of the finest firearms then available, besides fourteen hunting dogs. Our old friend Henry Chatillon, Parkman's guide, was here in the same capacity.

The overlord of all this train was a young Irish baronet, Sir George Gore, with an income of two hundred thousand dollars a year and an itch to spend it. Probably the mountain man, used to supporting himself with a rifle and a handful of "possibles," smiled when he first looked on this grand equipment. With the personalities, however, it was different. Gore and

Bridger took to each other immediately. Bridger was at once put on the payroll.

The winter at Laramie was followed by a long jaunt down the Powder River to the Yellowstone River and to Tongue River, where they wintered. The return journey was made by way of the Yellowstone and Missouri Rivers. The long evenings Gore spent in company with Bridger—the mountain man spinning his inimitable yarns to the Irish baronet; Gore reading to Bridger, keenly interested in the shrewd comments of the illiterate frontiersman. The chase was not neglected for Gore's bag included "forty grizzlies, twenty-five hundred buffaloes, elk, deer, antelope and other *small* game." This was the day of the slaughter-made sportsman, and a writer of that day compares Gore's record proudly with another individual who had become famous for killing big game in its hundreds in Africa.

Gore was a gold mine, which the people at every point he touched, hastened to harvest. The Irishman's indifference and patience gave out when finally on the return journey at Fort Union —formerly Fort Henry, the scene of Bridger's first winter as a trapper—they wanted him to pay an exorbitant amount for transporting his party and equipment. He burnt his whole train, and stood by until everything was consumed in the flames, so that the greedy ones should get no benefit whatever out of any salvage.

In 1859 the government sent Capt. W. F. Reynolds of the Engineering Corps, with fifteen scientists, to make a reconnaissance and survey of the Yellowstone River, and Jim Bridger was engaged to guide it. During this excursion, while crossing a small stream, Bridger discovered an outcropping of gold, and took a few samples of the ore to Reynolds. Reynolds pledged him immediately not to whisper a word of it, for he was afraid that all his men would desert him. It is interesting to recall here that Bridger had made other discoveries of gold; that some years previous he had shown Capt. Stansbury a number of outcroppings of coal—there was one near Fort Bridger that supplied him with fuel—and in Colorado he made a silver strike. He had known also in his mountain days of a petroleum flow, then merely a medicinal oil. None of these things seemed to have stirred him as a means to wealth—not even the gold, which had sent the great wave of emigrants rolling past his fort. It must have seemed too grubby a business to him, too confining for a man who wished to wander long and far. It was another generation than his that was to breed those scouts who would track small particles of float, and thin veins to their lair; who were to wander through great wastes and test their fortune with picks and dynamite.

Bridger told Reynolds of the region now known as Yellowstone Park, and the army officer was very anxious to see its wonders. Unfortunately for him he wanted to enter it from the west, and Bridger warned him that the snow in the spring would make it impossible to cross the passes. Sure enough the attempt they made failed, but Reynolds had enough of faith in what Bridger told him to put Yellowstone Lake and many other details, including the geyser valley he had not seen, into the map that was the result of the survey.

The year following his return from the Reynolds Expedition, Bridger piloted E. L. Berthoud in the survey of a route between Denver and Salt Lake City. In all these expeditions the trained topographers found that Bridger saved them not only an immense amount of time and trouble by being able to tell every foot of the country that lay before them, but his judgment was so good that if he was told the grade they wanted he could outline the whole route, so accurate was his memory. He never forgot a place if he had seen it once, and every detail of it would be photographed on his mind. An army officer says that when Bridger explained a route "he would describe it mile by mile—trees, rocks, grades, streams, everything."

His judgment was uncanny. He could guess the height of a mountain or a pass much more accurately than the trained surveyors. One of the anecdotes of the Berthoud survey is a dispute as to the height of two passes. Bridger said that one of them was between a thousand and two thousand feet lower than the other and invited the surveyors to "put their clocks on 'em." Sure enough the instruments showed that the difference was just fifteen hundred feet. Bridger was equally accurate in his estimates of the depth of a canyon. He would sometimes drop a stone, and estimate the depth within a few feet by counting. General Dodge sums up the testimony about him as a trail-breaker: "As a guide he was without an equal, and this is the testimony of every one who ever employed him. He was a born topographer; the whole west was mapped out in his mind, and such was his instinctive sense of locality and direction that it used to be said of him that he could smell his way where he could not see it."

There were a great many other minor journeys during these years. They are without sig-

nificance here, but there remains Bridger's part
in the third great highway of the west that was
laid out in these years—the Bozeman Trail.

Stories concerning his finding of gold on the
Reynolds expedition, and other rumors fell on
attentive ears, for this was a gold-crazy era.
Prospectors made a strike in Montana and there
was a rush of gold-seekers as soon as it was
known. A race developed between Bozeman
and Bridger with parties of gold-seekers bound
for what is now Virginia City in Montana.
Bridger followed a more southerly, and a little
longer route, than Bozeman. The advantage
was to neither one, for both trains arrived at
their destination about the same time.

In the rush for gold as we have noted in the
California business, and many of its tragedies,
the only route that a gold-crazy individual could
stand was the shortest one, and Bozeman's was
undoubtedly the most direct. But Bridger knew
it meant trouble, for it passed through the heart
of the Sioux country, and it was plain to any one
who knew their temper at the time that this was
asking for trouble. Only a chain of forts could
hold it safe for the traveler, and after a number
of gold seekers had lost their lives, including
Bozeman himself, this the government attempted
to supply. Bridger was chief scout for this ex-

pedition, and during the building and garrison-
ing of the stockades, he made a survey of the
Bozeman route from Fort Phil Kearney to the
gold fields, relocating a part of the trail. It was
abandoned four years after the route was first
opened, the traffic passing from Denver to Salt
Lake City and then north beyond the Sioux
country into Montana.

When Bridger took his train of gold seekers
to Montana in rivalry with Bozeman, he was
sixty years of age. His skin was now like wrin-
kled parchment. Gone was the figure described
as "straight as an arrow." The hardships of the
life he had been living for forty-two years were
telling on him, but there were still some years
of scouting and Indian-fighting ahead of him.

# CHAPTER XII

## MOUNTAIN MARRIAGE

SOMEWHERE during the gold rush days Jim Bridger bought a farm a few miles south of Kansas City, Missouri. It was a big farm, for Bridger was feeling wealthy. He purchased it to make a home for his children who were growing up. In the years of his health he visited there only occasionally.

Bridger married three times. His first wife was the daughter of a Flathead chief. Just when this marriage took place we do not know, probably when he was nearer forty than thirty. A great many trappers took Indian wives, white women leaving the romance of the mountains en-

tirely to their red sisters. Until the coming of
the emigrants the only white women who had
adventured into the mountains was the wife of
Manuel Lisa, who had journeyed part way into
them, accompanying her husband to his trading
post on the Yellowstone, the two missionary
ladies whose passing to Oregon we have noted,
and later one or two others also bound for the
missions. It almost seems as if, in the mountain
days, to marry a white woman was to cease to be
a mountain man. John Colter's marriage was
the end of his adventures; Ashley gave up his
interests in the mountains the year after he married; others, too, settled down in St. Louis as
soon as they had taken unto themselves a wife
among their own people. To the eastern cities
the Missouri settlements were the end of civilization, and in all truth that was hard enough;
the trapper's moving tipi would have been a terrible, if not impossible, life for the white woman.

The Indian woman had an advantage because
she knew no other home but the wilderness, and
her arts and accomplishments and philosophy
were suited to such living. But she also had a
heroic spirit and a book could be written about
the Indian heroines of the mountains who
were white men's wives. Sacajawea, the Bird
Woman, who guided and saved the Lewis and

Clark expedition, and Dorian's Sioux wife who accompanied the Astor Overlanders of 1811 were only the forerunners of a great number of brave and gallant Indian women who shared the lot of the mountain men. Both of the women we have mentioned bore children while on the trail.

What a life it was! The mountain man's wife had to share every danger of the trail, and to do much of its hard work. They cooked their men folks' meals, tanned the skins the traps yielded, made and broke camp, packed and attended to the transportation of the tipi or lodge, its long poles and the heavy buffalo skins that formed its cover. In the spring and fall hunts, almost every day was moving day. The Indian wife would also make the moccasins, the clothing, and such part of the trapper's equipment as was made with skin, often decorating them most artistically, and she would see that his lodge was comfortable with soft furs on which he could recline. Joe Meek, the trapper and Oregon settler to whom we have referred, had an Indian wife named the Mountain Lamb, who constantly traveled the trail with him. She had several narrow escapes from the Blackfeet, and finally the Bannock got her with an arrow in her heart. Washington Irving tells the story of one of Bridger's trappers, Loretto by name, who mar-

ried a Blackfoot girl whom he had ransomed
from the Crows, and whom Bridger took with
him as interpreter in the encounter with a Blackfoot chief which we have narrated. In the
mêlée, the Blackfoot dragged her off. Loretto
noticing her struggles to get back to him, caught
up their child, rushed across the bullet swept
ground and put the youngster in her arms. The
Blackfoot chief was touched by Loretto's devotion and sent him back unharmed, but refused
to let the girl go back with him. Loretto managed to get her back subsequently.

The mountains were full of stories of love-
struck Indian girls helping captive white men
to escape. There is such a legend concerning
Bridger being taken by the Blackfeet and escaping through the help of the chief's daughter,
who had fallen in love with him.

The free-trapper's wife was a person of importance. Coming into the summer rendezvous,
she, and the horse she rode, were decked out as
bravely as her husband, and much of his prodigal spending was for her adornment. As we
have suggested, however, Bridger's wooing was
later than that gay period; it is probable that he
married after the day of the rendezvous was
over.

These daughters of the forest trails had a romantic appeal all of their own. An impressionable youngster crossing the mountains in the covered wagon days jots the following down in his diary regarding an Indian tribe the train met with in the mountains:

"Among the party I noticed a very beautiful young female, the daughter of one of the chiefs of the party, who sat upon her horse with the ease and grace almost of a fairy. She was clothed in a buckskin shirt, pantaloons, and moccasins, with some really tasteful ornaments suspended around her neck and delicate wrist. It will be a long time before I forget the cheerful and attractive countenance, graceful figure, and vivacity of feature and language of this untutored child of nature."

On the other hand, Bonneville tells of the speech a trapper made to an Indian chief on asking him to choose for him a wife. He did not want a "young, giddy-pated girl, that will think of nothing but flaunting and finery, but a sober, discreet, hard-working squaw; one that will share my lot without flinching, however hard it may be; that can take care of my lodge and be a companion and helpmate to me in the wilderness."

In the Indian tribes marriage was a simple matter, consisting merely of the smoking of the pipe all round, a few admonitions from the chief to the bride on the duties of a good squaw, presents bestowed on the family, and of the girl moving in and taking charge of the lodge of her husband. The very simplicity with which the matter was conducted led the white man sometimes to hold its responsibilities lightly, but on the whole they showed a commendable devotion both to their Indian wives and to the children of such marriages.

Bridger's Flathead Indian wife died in 1846, leaving him three children, two girls and a boy. The eldest girl he sent to Whitman's mission school near Walla Walla, where she lost her life in the Indian massacre of that station.

The year after his first wife's death he married a Ute Indian girl, who died in child-birth. Bridger nursed this child, Virginia, on buffalo milk.

His third wife, a Snake chief's daughter, he married in 1850. Of this lady we have a number of pen pictures made by people who passed through Fort Bridger, who speak of her hospitality and her kindness to them. Mrs. Ferris, whose comment on Bridger we have quoted, says that Bridger introduced them to his wife and showed them his children (probably only the last two) whom she describes as "keen, bright-eyed little things." There were two children by the third marriage, the last born on the Little Santa Fe farm that Bridger had bought. A writer states that Bridger "was as careful of his half-breed children as any parent on the borders of civilization could be." All except the first, and the youngest children who were brought up on the farm, were sent to school in St. Louis. The eldest boy, Felix, fought in the Civil War, and was commissioned as an officer in the Artillery. Virginia married an army officer. None of the children except Virginia long survived their father.

When Bridger had the idea of purchasing the farm he did not, of course, have the money in cash, or bills, or a bank account. In trading such as Bridger and Vasquez conducted at their fort, the business was one of constant exchange of one thing for another. The emigrant finding himself in need of something—a horse, cattle, blankets, clothing—would look over Bridger's store which usually included buffalo robes, and the skins tanned and worked by Indian squaws into clothes, moccasins, and would bargain for what he wanted in terms of the surplus of something he carried—flour, bacon, powder, lead, wool blankets, knives, spirits, hats, ready-made clothes, coffee, sugar—in a word, any article or articles from a wagon to the smallest thing he carried. Similarly Bridger traded with Indians and trappers, and the final wealth was counted very much in furs.

On the occasion of the farm-buying journey, Bridger packed in five thousand beaver skins and some other fur. For once business was breaking right for the mountain man. There had been a slump in beaver, for in the big cities silk was taking the place of beaver fur in the high hat, but now the market took a sudden rise and Bridger was able to exchange his beaver for seven dollars a pelt; the other fur brought five thousand dollars more, so that he found himself with forty thousand dollars in actual cash as his share of the trading.

Although Bridger bought this farm and later a house in near-by Westport from Col. A. G. Boone, the mountains were still his home. To him towns were gloomy canyons, and the ways of its inhabitants a contradiction of everything in life he loved. He once said he had walked the streets of a town and seen a thousand men, not one of whom had invited him to "come into his lodge and eat." For him that was a symbol of life in the wilderness.  There every one you met was either friend or foe.  If the former you pressed every comfort and luxury you had on him; if the latter you cocked your rifle and went to it with as ardent a spirit.

# CHAPTER XIII

## "HERE LIES BRIDGER"

BRIDGER'S contacts with the many famous civilians and the military men who were mapping out the new country, brought into focus a quality in him that was outstanding—a rare sense of humor. There was a certain gallantry to it, for he used it to turn the concern regarding his hardships to a smile. His modesty used it to parry both the curious and the hero-worshiping. The peculiar imagination of the Bridger story when it dealt with natural phenomena set a fashion in that type of exaggeration.

Men like Stansbury, Gunnison, Father De

Smet and others, who fell under the spell of Jim Bridger, mentioned him with admiration in their writing, and talked of the things he had told them regarding the natural wonders he had found in the mountains. He had been for years a fabulous figure among the mountain men; now the settlements, reading of him in the books, began to take an interest in him. Consequently, Bridger coming into Kansas City in 1853 on a visit to his family, found that the editor of the Kansas City Journal wanted to learn of those wonders direct from him, particularly about the phenomena of the Yellowstone. Bridger answered his questions faithfully and accurately. Before writing the story, or as one account has it, after setting it up, the editor asked a man who claimed he knew Bridger and the mountains of the truth of what he had been told. This man was positive. He warned the editor that he would be laughed out of town if he printed "any of Jim Bridger's lies," and so the material was killed, although the laugh turned out to be on the other side.

We cannot fully understand Bridger's humor unless we realize that it was a tonic that was born in the grim hazards of the mountain days when every trail held its dangers. To endure them year after year one had to laugh at them.

To Bridger a fight was only a "squall"; to his men the persistent Blackfeet were the "Bugs Boys"; an arrow was nothing—somebody "butchered" it out. Having a man or two killed was part of the routine, and one had to grow callous to stand it. A certain grimness also crept into the mountain man's outlook on life. One of the anecdotes, illustrating that attitude, concerns a thunderstorm when a bolt of lightning struck the encampment of Fraeb, one of the Rocky Mountain Company's partners. At the moment Fraeb rushed in, and seeing a man lying dead shouted: "By Gott, who did shoot Gutherie?" A trapper answered indifferently: "God a'mighty. I expect he's afiring into camp." Bridger's stories were cheery yarns, full of humor and imagination, a tonic for nerves and muscles under constant strain.

Capt. Humfreville, in the rigors of an Indian campaign, and feeling very blue, acknowledges his obligation to Bridger, whose stories cheered him up from day to day. Bridger never used his stories for magnifying his personal adventures, as the free-trapper was reputed to do. A man who knew him says: "He never in my presence vaunted himself about his personal actions. He never told about how brave he was, nor how many Indians he had killed." Bridger never let his sense of humor mislead or inconvenience any one he had anything to do with. Engineer Berthoud remarks: "When Bridger was consulted as to facts he was truth itself." He was not a practical joker. He told his stories for entertainment, and they were labeled fiction so plainly that anybody but a fool knew it for what it was.

He told his stories with a straight, solemn face, seeming to be in deadly earnest, and with great skill. A standard question of the tenderfoot to the weather-worn mountain men would be, "How long have you been in the mountains?" A standard reply was that when the trapper first came there all the mountains were valleys. Bridger handled the idea a little differently. He would start on a semi-philosophic basis suggesting the probability that since animals and trees and every living thing grew, the same was probably true of the hills and rocks. Working down gradually to the peaks they could see that now seemed larger, to the passes he had crossed that now seemed higher, and the rocks that now seemed to bulge out more prominently, he would get his listener carried away with the theme, until finally the auditor would assert his reason and suggest that Bridger was deceiving himself with the idea. Then Bridger would clinch the

argument, in deadly seriousness, by pointing, as
he once did, to Court House Rock, and asking:
did his listener know what that had once been?
Deceived by his acting, and expecting to hear
something interesting the reply would be a
prompt, "No. Please tell us." Well, Bridger
would tell him: Court House Rock was once a
stone he threw at a jack-rabbit!

This idea was varied to fit the thought that
was uppermost in his listener's mind. Thus to a
settler or a farmer interested in the fertility of
the soil, his illustration of that quality in the land
made Independence Rock the lusty descendant
of a stone he threw across the Sweetwater.

Indian fighting, of course, provided a constant theme. Even in the fifties, Bridger's adventures among the Indians marked him as a
hero of a hundred exploits, and his fame was
known along every foot of the long trail. Naturally enough every tenderfoot, whether soldier,
settler or emigrant, would ask him questions
about those experiences. There does not come
down to us a single instance of his speaking
about his doughty deeds as a warrior, and from
the "Bridger Stories" that deal with Indian
fighting it appears that he had an actual dislike
for talking of himself at all in the rôle of hero.
The most celebrated of these Indian stories

would be varied as to beginning, but always
come to the same ending. In brief, this is one
form in which it would run.

Bridger and a companion laying their trap
lines were suddenly attacked by a band of about
sixty Indians. They were game and made a
fight of it, bringing down no less than twenty
redskins. Then they decided to run.

It was a long and thrilling chase. Finally, at
nightfall, they made the shelter of some woods.
They felt safe, for it is well known that Indians
never attack after dark. But whatever hopes
they had of resting themselves was soon dispelled, for the Indians attacked them again, and
Bridger and his companion, exhausted though
they were, were forced to put up another fight.
No less than twenty more Indians bit the dust
before they were able to disengage and run for
it again.

They slipped into a canyon with the war-
whoop ringing on their back trail, and speeded
along the ravine, the Indians in hot pursuit.
They had to keep on, although the Indians were
gaining on them, for the walls of the canyon rose
in a sheer precipice, which it was impossible to
scale. Then suddenly in front of them loomed
a waterfall three hundred feet high. Right, left
and forward there was no way of escape, and

the Indians were every moment drawing closer.

The story so far is plainly labeled fiction to any one who knew anything about frontier conditions. No white men lived who could make a running fight with Indians on those terms; and no Indians ever existed who would sacrifice forty scalps in the hope of getting two. But the British army officer, seeing America's wildest west, who had the honor of hearing the story in this form, looked up from the notes he was making in his little book, and asked breathlessly:

"Tell me, Mr. Bridger, how did you escape?"

Bridger eyed him solemnly and drawled: "We didn't, Mister. They killed us both."

Bridger had a number of animal stories. One of them, a bear story, provided a phrase which in later years army officers delighted in using to describe the condition of fellow-officers who were at a loose end. As usual he would lead up to his story perhaps by a discussion of the habits of these animals, or better still of how plentiful they had been in the early days in the mountains. Once in those days, Bridger's story would run, he had found a nice little glade where he set about preparing a meal. When he looked up there were bears all over the place, two hundred and fifty of them, sitting under the trees and looking down at him.

There the story would end. The puzzled listener seeing that no more was forthcoming would ask:

"Well, what did you do?"

"Oh, didn't do nothing."

"Well, what did the bears do?"

"Oh, they didn't do nothing. Jest sat around."

The mountains were not without their jokes on Jim Bridger, and those who knew him loved to tell of his being disconcerted. Once in the Blackfoot country an Indian ambushed him. The brave had a running shot, for Bridger was mounted. The arrow was fortunately not as well aimed as it might have been. It missed Bridger, but drove into the flank of his horse. The animal plunged immediately, then started to kick and cut up generally. Bridger, riding as usual with his rifle across the pommel of his saddle, was taken completely off guard. He managed to keep his seat, but lost his gun. Before he brought his horse under control, the Blackfoot was running for the rifle, and Bridger seeing that he had no chance to recover it, headed his horse at a gallop for the camp. The following day while inspecting the rifles of his men, he came across one, the property of an Irishman, that was dirty. These inspections were always strict, so Bridger rebuked him, asking: "What would you do if the Blackfeet attacked us?" "Begorra," came the Irishman's pat reply, "I'd throw me rifle to them and run the same as you did!"

Whether Bridger fined him, as was the custom, or not we do not know. It's not unlikely, for on another occasion a trapper came to him and criticized the camp Bridger had chosen, stating that its position at the foot of some hills could not be defended even against unarmed men. Bridger maintained that it was a good camp, and that he had picked it with its defence in mind. The trapper thereupon went into the hills and rolled a bowlder over. The force of the tumbling bowlder was spent before it reached the camp, but there was enough motion in it to bump into a tipi, break a rifle, and hit a Frenchman. Bridger docked the trapper for the damage to the rifle and the lodge, as well as ten dollars for the Frenchman's shin. His command made a rime about it:

> The rock rushed down with a mighty din,
> And broke a gun and a Frenchman's shin.

Capt. Humfreville tells of a joke on Bridger that he had a part in. During one winter encampment while scouting for the Army,

Bridger's buckskins contracted lice. This was no new thing for the mountain men, for their long one-suit marches brought this condition about frequently. Every skin bought from the Indians was full of the little animals and they had to be most carefully dispossessed. In spring, summer or fall, nature provided a delousing station. The trapper would strip clean and place all his garments on an antheap. The busy little insects would in a short while eat them clean of all the vermin. Nothing like that being at hand, Bridger asked Humfreville if he knew any remedy. The latter said he would fix it, poured powder along the seams, and set fire to it. The suit, of course, was a wreck, and Bridger was so mad that Humfreville was afraid for a little while that Bidger would keep his threat and kill him. Bridger had to go about wrapped in a buffalo robe until a new pair of buckskins was made for him.

But to continue with the Bridger story. Most of his mountain yarns had their basis in some natural phenomena that he had observed. Thus he told a story of a great snow that had raged over the Salt Lake Valley for seventy days, as a result of which a vast herd of buffalo had frozen to death. All he had to do was to push them into the Great Salt Lake and for years he was

able to feed the Ute nation with the salted buffalo meat. Actually in his time there were several winters in the mountains so severe that
hundreds of wild animals froze to death; and
the waters of Great Salt Lake are so salt that
meat left in them for twelve hours becomes
corned beef; in twenty-four hours it becomes so
salt that it is almost unpalatable.

The gold-crazy hordes, asking for information that might help them to find it in the mountains, led him to tell a story of a great diamond.
Chased by Indians he had hidden during daylight, and traveled at night by the light it re-
flected! Icicles shining in the winter sun, or
some similar thing might have suggested it.
Bridger said that one man actually believed in
the existence of the great diamond.

The obsidian cliff and the crystal mountain
gave him the basis for a variety of stories. One
form of it was that while out hunting he had seen
an elk. He fired, but the elk paid no attention
either to his bullet or the report of the rifle. He
fired again, with the same result. Thereupon he
investigated and found that he had been shooting at an animal he was seeing through a glass
mountain!

A boiling spring, gushing over into Yellowstone Lake, and forming a little pool on the

surface where it boiled and bubbled on top of the cold water, gave him an idea for a fish story. His yarn was that he let a line down there, caught his fish, and had it ready cooked on its journey to the air.

The curious delayed echo of one mountain, gave him a story of a place where he used to camp. The echo returned after five or six hours, so he turned it into a first-rate alarm clock. When going to bed he would shout, "Time to get up." The echo would wake him at the proper time in the morning.

The Fire Hole River, whose waters, though icy cold on top are warm at the bottom as it passes over the hot bed under the stream, provided the basis for a story Bridger told of a river whose course was so swift that friction heated the water that rubbed against the rocky bottom, while the water on top remained cold.

Around the petrified forests there were, of course, many Indian legends. Bridger's own stories concerning them were of a place in which not only trees were petrified, but the sage bushes, sage hens, birds on the wing, even their song, the animals, fruit, moonlight and sunlight, even the law of gravitation. As a concession to the gold seekers, the bushes later began to bear berries of precious stones.

Some of the things he saw seemed like fiction in that day, even when presented as fact. The geysers, for instance, or Two Ocean Pass, which he discovered. Here, eight thousand one hundred feet above sea level, two streams come out of opposite sides from the mountains. Each divides into two forks. One fork of each stream waters the Atlantic; the other the Pacific. The fish often swim from one ocean waterway into the other.

The army surveyors Stansbury, Gunnison and Reynolds, whom Bridger guided, and many other men of intelligence to whom he spoke regarding these wonders of the Yellowstone believed him, and what they wrote shows how careful and accurate he was when dealing with facts. Here is Gunnison's account of what Bridger described to him: "A lake sixty miles long, cold and pellucid, embossed amid high and precipitous mountains, on the west side in a sloping plain several miles wide, with clumps of trees and groves of pines. The ground resounds to the tread of horses. Geysers spurt up seventy feet high, with a terrific hissing noise at regular intervals. Waterfalls are sparkling, leaping and thundering down the precipice, and collect in the pool below. The river issues from the lake, and for fifteen miles roars through the perpendicular canyon at the outlet. In this section are the Great Springs, so hot that meat is readily cooked in them, and as they descend on the successive terraces, offer delightful baths. On the other side is an acid spring, which gushes out in a river torrent; and below is a cave which supplies vermilion for the savages in abundance."

Father De Smet retold Bridger's description of Yellowstone as follows: "Bituminous, sulphurous and boiling springs are very numerous in it. The hot springs contain a large quantity of calcareous matter . . . the earth is thrown up very high, and the influence of the elements causes it (geysers) to take the most varied and the most fantastic shapes. . . . Gas, vapor and smoke are continually escaping by a thousand spring openings from the base to the summit of the volcanic pile; the noise at times resembles the steam let off by a boat."

Some twelve years after the Kansas City editor had shelved his account of the wonders of Yellowstone, Bridger told it to a man who owned the train that he had convoyed into Montana. This gentleman, N. P. Langford, when Bridger told him that he had seen a column of water, as thick as a man's body, spout a hundred feet into the air and keep doing it at regular intervals, reasoned that since in all the world such natural phenomena were not found outside of the geyser springs in Iceland, it was unlikely that Bridger had heard of them, and argued that Bridger's accounts rested on something more solid than simple imagination.

Langford organized a party that in 1870 explored a part of the region—it is a huge area larger than the states of Rhode Island and Delaware put together. He and his companions were men of standing. Later Langford induced the government to set it aside as a public park and became its first superintendent.

The amusing sequel to Langford's exploration is .this: In the year following his return he wrote a number of articles on what the expedition had seen. These articles were published in a New York magazine. The editor received a great number of letters criticizing his gullibility for having accepted the story and printing it, one of them remarking, "This man Langford must be the champion liar of the northwest!"

# PART IV

## CHIEF SCOUT

## CHAPTER XIV

### "The Destroying Angels"

IN June of 1847, Jim Bridger riding to the
settlements for supplies for his trading post
encountered the outriders of a train making
its way into the mountains. There were the
usual greetings and questions as party met party
on the great trail. Who was the mountain man,
they asked. Jim Bridger. Not Colonel Bridger
of Fort Bridger? That was the very man they
wanted to see. Would he talk with their
leaders? There were a thousand questions they
would like to ask him. It was just about five
o'clock in the evening, and there were several
hours of daylight left in which to travel, but it

was never Jim Bridger's way to let his business convenience interfere with helping anybody out. He offered to pull up his train and camp it with theirs overnight, and both parties were turned out of the trail about a mile and a half to make camp.

Whether Jim Bridger had heard of the Mormons then we do not know. In any case it would have mattered little to him. What he saw of their encampment, and what he learned of their tactics, must have impressed him, for it was organized with sound commonsense. The one hundred and forty-three men who made up the party (there were three women and two children besides) conducted themselves with semi-military precision. There were captains of fifties and captains of tens. They made and broke camp to the sound of a bugle. On the march the wagons, some seventy of them, advanced two abreast, each with a man walking by its side. Rifles were never left unloaded. There was a small cannon on wheels too. In the presence of Indians the wagons were drawn up five abreast as they advanced, and the boom of the cannon rolling over the prairie was sufficient to prevent any hostile demonstration. Their stock was pastured under guard, and at night driven within the semicircle or circle of wagons drawn up wheel to wheel. Their wagons were loaded with ploughs, seed, grain; they had plenty of ammunition. They had some scientific instruments, and were making a record of their observations. Every ten miles they set up wooden trail-markers to guide those coming behind them. (The forty-niners burned these up for firewood). All in all they must have impressed Bridger as one of the most competent trains that had made its way into the mountains.

Bridger spent a long time with the "Twelve," and later dined with Brigham Young, the chief leader, on a table on which was spread a white cloth; there was bread, too—luxuries he had not seen for many years. If Young told him what they were doing, Bridger must have been both impressed and touched with the almost epic quality of their undertaking. The Mormons, in their seventeen years' history had fallen into violent disagreement with almost every neighboring community where they had settled. They had moved from New York State to Ohio to Missouri to Illinois. In the last named state they had at first prospered greatly around their settlement at Nauvoo, but as at every other place where they had settled bitter quarrels arose between them and the "gentiles." In Illinois the feeling eventually ran so high that a mob killed

Joseph Smith, their prophet, while he was under the governor's protection, and practically forced the Mormons to abandon their city, their farms and their homes.

Everything they owned had been sold, the proceeds turned into wagons and equipment, and fifteen thousand people were moving westward, the advance party building camps for those that followed to occupy; sowing crops in the spring that those coming behind should reap in the fall. Men worked along the route as laborers and artisans, often taking their pay in farm produce. It was an experience not without terrible sufferings, especially when the aged and the infirm were forced to stand the rigors of the winter and when sickness became epidemic among them. Hundreds perished from these causes.

Brigham Young, the leader of the Mormon Church, was a man two or three years Bridger's senior. As a young man he had worked at odd jobs as carpenter, painter and glazier. He had little formal schooling. After his conversion to Mormonism, he rose so rapidly in its counsels that at the Prophet's death he came swiftly to the undisputed leadership of the church. He was leading his people now to the west, the promised land. Just where he would find it he did not know, but he was certain he would recognize it when he saw it.

Brigham Young was attracted by General Fremont's description of the Salt Lake Valley, which the "Pathfinder" had first seen (as Bridger had done some seventeen or eighteen years before him) from the top of a hill. The general had been impressed by what he saw and compared the thrill he felt to Balboa's view of the Pacific, "upon that peak in Darien." The Mormon party had one of Fremont's maps with them—a map not without its inaccuracies. Brigham Young had talked of this valley to two experienced mountain men he had met on the trail before coming up with Bridger, but both had done their best to discourage his settling there, one of them even offering to take him to another part of the mountains, but failed to show up at the time agreed.

Bridger had an entirely different attitude to the Salt Lake Valley. He not only knew it better than any man living, but it had been a region that had fascinated him. The journal of one of the Mormon leaders—Clayton—shows that Bridger gave them detailed and reliable information, telling them what the Indians grew and where; marking the course of rivers, woods, canyons; describing the soil as fertile but pointing out that in the uplands the early frosts would make it difficult to grow corn. He described the entire country to them as far as the Sierras, and south towards Mexico; the different kinds of trees they would find, and where the Indians raised corn and wheat. He mentioned places where they would find outcroppings of coal. There is a popular Mormon legend that Bridger offered a thousand dollars for an ear of corn that was grown in the Salt Lake Valley. There is no reason why Bridger, whose experiments with agriculture could have been at the best only limited, should have been dogmatic; or why the Mormons, who had been so willing to be guided elsewhere should have felt so sure of themselves. Clayton reports Bridger as saying, "the soil is good, and likely to produce corn were it not for the excessive cold nights, which he thinks would prevent the growth of corn."

The meeting ended with the utmost cordiality, which endured for two or three years, Bridger's partner Vasquez moving into Salt Lake City and setting up a store there.

The instinct that turned the Mormons into Salt Lake Valley was to make them the best desert farmers in the world, and the pioneers of irrigation. The first years were hard—drought, a plague of locusts and grasshoppers, all the

trials familiar to our "dry" farmers to-day they
had to face in those first years. That they survived so well and prospered was due in large
measure to the gold discovery in California.
Thousands came pouring through the Mormon country—selling everything the Mormons
needed, at bargain prices, buying everything the
Mormons had to sell, at a tremendous advance.

Brigham Young's own power was increasing
each day. He was head of the church, to which
every Mormon turned over one-tenth of his income. He had many business enterprises. He
was made Governor when Utah was declared a
territory, and as his Bishops were the local mag-
istrates, he was, in effect, the law. He was also
made Indian agent, so that he held in his hands
almost despotic powers.

In 1849 Bridger sent word to Young that the
Utes were planning mischief—troubles that resulted in Lt. Gunnison some time later losing
his life. There was no conflict between Bridger
and the Mormons until competition for the emigrant trade brought the Mormon concessionaires
to trading with the emigrants along the great
trail, far from their own basin. Bridger was
getting a large share of this around his fort, and
with a few other mountain men was proving a

thorn in the flesh of Mormon traders seeking to win it.

These conflicts led finally to affidavits being sworn out against Bridger that he was selling powder and lead to the Indians. A warrant was issued, and a marshal with a posse of one hundred and fifty Danites, "The Destroying Angels" of many encounters with the gentiles of Missouri and Illinois, rode out to take Bridger prisoner and confiscate his dangerous goods. They expected the mountain man to put up a fight and made sure of the odds. It was regarded not as a case of arresting a single man; they paid Bridger the compliment of regarding it as a movement of a regular expeditionary force. Salt Lake City was in a high state of excitement for weeks.

Bridger declined the unequal combat. The Destroying Angels could not find him. They looted the fort and its stock and set fire to a portion of it. They made a pretense of withdrawing and set an ambush, but Bridger was not to be caught by any such trick. After a while they gave up, returning in triumph to the city for had they not "spoiled the gentile"?

Bridger claimed his loss was worth a hundred thousand dollars. Shortly after the Danites finally withdrew Bridger got a surveyor who was present in the neighborhood, John M. Hockaday, to make a survey of the land he had occupied, nearly four thousand acres, which he sent to Washington to be filed with the Land Office. The Mormons subsequently made several efforts to settle this part of the country, but without success.

There was slim hope that any restitution would be made to Bridger, and, indeed, none was made. But the tactics the Mormon power used in dealing with him, they used in other dealings with the gentiles, and in doing so brought a great deal of trouble on themselves. The non-Mormon territorial officers and judges appointed by the Federal Government found conditions so menacing that they fled Utah for their lives. The California emigrants found that the Mormon powers demanded a permit from them to enter and leave its territory; taxed them for the goods they brought in and for the goods they took out. They also charged the Mormons with the murder of emigrants and stated that it was impossible for a gentile to obtain justice in the Mormon courts. Early in 1857 Bridger went to Washington to present his own grievance and was introduced by a Missouri senator to President Buchanan.

Whatever Bridger had to say to the President

could have had little bearing on the only possible outcome of matters in Utah territory. The Federal authority had been defied, and there was no course open but to assert that authority. President Buchanan ordered the army to occupy the territory, and appointed a new Governor, Mr. Alfred Cumming. A force consisting of three columns under the command of Colonel, later General, Albert Sidney Johnston, totalling fifteen hundred men, was ordered to Utah. The first column consisting of the supply train, strung out in small detachments, was met by Mormon patrols with orders to destroy the wagons and run off the stock, but not to attack the men. They carried out their orders well, destroying a great deal of the supplies. General Johnston, with Bridger acting as guide and scout, did not leave Laramie until October 5th and made the journey to Fort Bridger in less than a month, the severe weather that had set in taking heavy toll of their stock. The third column, starting later, had even greater hardships to face.

An advance in the winter was impossible and General Johnston decided to encamp near Fort Bridger until spring cleared the roads. To resupply himself with horses, he sent Capt. Randolph B. Marcy with a small body of men to

New Mexico. This column made an epic journey in the dead of winter across the Uinta Mountains, through blinding storms and passes piled high with snow, bringing back in the spring fifteen hundred horses and mules and an escort of five companies of infantry and mounted riflemen.

From the moment the federal troops set out there was a great deal of chest-thumping among the Mormons (their population had by now grown to about fifty thousand), to the general effect that rather than permit the occupation of the country by federal troops they would fight to the last man and destroy everything they possessed. They took a much more sober view, however, as matters approached a show-down. They made advances to the new Governor, received him well, and stipulated a peace which would keep the army outside of Utah territory. This Governor Cumming was agreeable to, but General Johnston construed his orders were to occupy the territory. When Johnston began marching, Brigham Young backed down, this time stipulating that the army should not encamp closer than forty miles to Salt Lake City, but Johnston marched his men there and pitched his camp within the city limits. It was a bloodless war, for not a shot was fired on either side.

Bridger asked to be discharged at Salt Lake City. His first experience as army scout had ended tamely, although his services as guide had saved General Johnston many hardships during the march.

While the expedition was encamped at his fort, Bridger agreed to rent it to the War Department for the sum of six hundred dollars a year for ten years, with an option to buy it during that period for ten thousand dollars. The officer drawing up the agreement very properly specified that the money was to be paid on Bridger establishing his title to the land to the satisfaction of the Quartermaster General. When Bridger and Vasquez first occupied this land it was Mexican territory. Mexican law specified that land so occupied was granted a title after ten years, and Bridger and Vasquez filed a preliminary claim with that government. When the territory passed into the possession of the United States, the government undertook to protect such claims. As we have seen Bridger filed his claim to the land with the U. S. Land Office in March, 1854. He had set up buildings on it in 1843. Bridger had no title, but his claim to such title was clear enough.

For the next ten years he was ranging the mountains and plains far and wide, chiefly as a government scout. When he got round to seeing about payments for this little business transaction he found that the War Department, standing on the letter of the law, would allow him nothing on the grounds that he could not actually produce title in writing. On this basis, at the time, they could have dispossessed three-fourths of the landholders in the territory of Utah. Congress eventually introduced a bill to pay Bridger six thousand dollars for the improvements on the land the government had taken over, but by the time they got around to passing the bill it had to be amended so that the payment could be made to his heirs, for the old scout had long been dead.

## CHAPTER XV

### THE WAR PIPE

THERE was an interval of several years before Bridger was again to serve the army as a scout, this time not against the white man but the Indian. Although they have been absent from our narrative of Bridger's trail-breaking years, Indians continued to play an immense part in his life. The Mountain Indians—the Snakes, Utes, Nez Perces, Flatheads, Crows and others—came gradually to look on him as one of their own, a respected and honored chief. Men like Stansbury and Gunnison and others were amazed by his powerful influence over the mountain tribes and

222

recommended him as the one man the government should name as Indian agent.

The stormy petrels of the Indian tribes were now the plains Indians, and especially the Sioux, Cheyennes and Arapahoes. The former especially had been steadily encroaching on the hunting grounds of the mountain tribes. They grew restless and hostile as the emigrants began to flow in a great tide through their hunting grounds, but the first bad feeling was quickly allayed in a statesmanlike way by a treaty following a conference of the tribes arranged by our old friend Fitzpatrick, who had been appointed an Indian agent. Jim Bridger was consulted about the making of this treaty, and took part in it as a leader of the Snakes. The Indians agreed to cease hostilities along the Overland route, and in return received fifty thousand dollars. This was one of the most effective agreements made with the Indians and brought a long peace.

The Indians' chief complaint had been that the emigrants were killing the game or driving it away, so that it was increasingly difficult for them to hunt the buffalo on which they depended for food, clothing and shelter. Now the rapid development of the mountain country and plains began to multiply those difficulties a hundredfold. The emigrant trade attracted numbers of men who began to set up ranches along the Overland and Oregon routes. Then came the discovery of gold in Colorado, Idaho, and finally Montana. People passing beyond their lands was one thing; people settling all around them was quite another. Into Colorado alone, in just one year during the gold strike one hundred and fifty thousand people entered.

The man in search of gold followed it to any place he thought he could find it. Gold-seeker or emigrant, the white man made no distinction between Indian and Indian. The Indian seldom distinguished between white man and white man. The emigrant who had a few horses run off by an Indian took it out of the first Indian he met. The Indian, if he considered himself badly treated by one white man, revenged himself on the next he saw. It is easy to see that with the best will in the world, under the conditions of white men pouring into the Indian country, conflicts would arise. Many white men considered themselves, at least in respect to the Indians, subject to no will but their own; Indian chiefs had only a loose control of their young braves and various chiefs of the same tribe acted quite independent of each other. Even if the white men could tell tribe from tribe, there was no certainty of the feelings of the different bands. To-day a Cheyenne band that was met might be brimming over with friendliness for the whites; to-morrow a band, also Cheyennes, were more than ready to be mean.

Despite these natural difficulties the west was developing fast, and with a minimum of conflict, when the Civil War in 1861 divided the country into North and South and plunged them at each other's throats. By this time the California and Pike's Peak Pony Express had given place to the daily overland stage, and the telegraph was humming messages across the continent. Soon branch lines of these services ran to Denver, and the foundation of many lines of intercommunication between western centers were laid, along which trains of supplies moved, for the new country was still dependent on the east for many of the essentials of life. There were small garrisons of government troops strung out in forts over the plains.

The Civil War seems to have made no impression whatever on the plains Indians. In 1862 the Indian country was still peaceful, though every little while there would be a raid. In this year we get a glimpse of Bridger convoying a U. S. federal judge, with an escort of troops, to Utah. Bridger's scouting experiences, like the other facts concerning his life, come down to us as though bits of a twenty-reel motion picture had been snipped out and miraculously saved, while the rest of the film was lost. These scenes, saved to us by chance, give us fortunately an indication of his caliber as a scout against the Indians, and some of the methods he employed. On this occasion, the government troops passing an emigrant train were informed that one of the wagons had straggled while on the march and had been set upon by Indians. Bridger and twenty soldiers rode in the direction indicated, and came upon the wagon destroyed and looted, and the occupants killed. One youngster who was dead had his hand clenched over a revolver, which the Indians had tried without success to release from its death-grip. Bridger when he saw the revolver began to make a cast in widening circles around the wagon until finally he came across a spot of blood in the sage and tall grass where one Indian had been wounded. He read the sign on the ground to mean that the raid had been made by twenty Arapahoes and Cheyennes, that they were well-mounted and their horses in good condition, that they had crossed the river and that there was no hope of catching up with them. A small party of soldiers were, however, detached to follow the trail, but failed

to come up with the raiders, although they followed it for five or six days.

We have a later glimpse of the method he
used when convoying a train through hostile
country. It was the same old caution of mountain days, making sure of the night's story on
the ground first of all. On the march he rode
far in advance of the train, making sure of the
country through which it would pass, sometimes
sending it a signal to corral for Indian attack.
He was frequently too far away to make the
camp before the Indians came riding down on
it. A youngster who was on the trains Bridger
escorted into Montana, says that he was always
fearful for the old man, caught out of the train
on these raids, but that each evening Bridger
would come jogging back at camping time se-
rene and unconcerned.

It was not until 1863 that the Indians' hand
began to be felt along the great trails and the
plains country. There seems to be a general
agreement that it was a near-sighted policy that
forced the Indians into acting with a semblance
of a virtue they never possessed, unity. A few
military fire-eaters, anxious to prove themselves
Indian fighters saw fit to revenge raids by attacking every Indian encampment they found.
As friendly Indians often proved the nearest at

hand, such gasconading tactics fell frequently on the least guilty, and it was not long before the whole country was seething with hostiles, though at the worst, there was little concerted action even by the Arapahoes, Cheyennes and Sioux bands. Indians were always willing to take service against other tribes, frequently their own, the Pawnees, Omaha, Crows and other Indians, especially the scouts of the first named tribe under Capt. Frank North, doing excellent service in the troubles that followed.

Gathering men for war, or even for raiding, in an Indian tribe was a complicated business, because each brave was so strongly individualistic that he had first to be won as a volunteer and then held by a series of successes that kept his loyalty. This loose discipline often showed itself in the impatience which destroyed the plans of a crafty leader. If heavy casualties were inflicted nothing could hold them, unless some special circumstances made them desperate. Relations were even more complicated when chief dealt with chief or tribe with tribe. An invitation to make war jointly would come in the form of a war pipe. The manner in which this was smoked would indicate whether the invitation was accepted, the braves in turn would join or refuse to join in the same way. When

they went to war in 1863 they did not so much
act together, as an army has one general who
directs the whole force; they began to act all at
the same time, raiding, burning and plundering
everything that appeared nearest their hand. It
is estimated that in that year a thousand whites
lost their lives.

The following year matters went from bad to
worse. It cost the government thirty million
dollars to repair the damage caused by Indian
raids. The whole country between the Arkansas River and the North Platte was ravaged by
the hostiles. Every ranch house and store was
looted and burned. Wagon trains and stage
coaches caught along the route were attacked
and destroyed. One stage coach captured had
an army paymaster as passenger. He escaped
into a near-by fort, abandoning the money he
carried for the soldiers' pay. The Indians,
breaking open the box, found the money, but as
it was all in bills they did not know it was of any
value. They scattered the greenbacks over the
prairie. One brave chopping a bundle of them
into four pieces, shouted gleefully as he tossed
them up in the air and watched the wind scatter
them far and wide. When the Indians withdrew
the paymaster had a search party on the prairie,
but did not succeed in recovering half his money.

The telegraph line when it was being strung out had fascinated the Indians, especially when they were told that it carried messages, and some of the chiefs were given a demonstration of its powers. General Dodge says that in the early days Indians could frequently be seen putting their ears to the poles and listening fascinated to the hum made by the wind striking the wires. They were surprised to find that General Dodge could not tell them what it said, especially as he would sometimes tell them the messages he was sending and receiving when he cut into the line with his field instruments. Whatever awe they first had was now worn by familiarity. They proceeded to tear down the line and burn the poles, destroying the system for hundreds of miles. The entire transportation and communication system came to a standstill, and there was fear even that the Santa Fe train would be forced to cease operations.

When General Dodge took over command of the entire region in 1864 he says that all the troops were behind stockades, the Indians having defeated them in every fight. The commanders of the three divisions in this territory gave him equally gloomy reports of their ability to do anything to stay the depredations or guard the territory not yet affected, one of the commanders stating: "I predict that if more troops are not sent into this district immediately the road will be stripped of every ranch and white man on it."

The Indian was master of quick marches, surprise attacks and cunning ambuscades. Under cover or in the open, riding his ponies like the wind, he was a warrior without an equal. His genius was quick attack or retreat. He had no stomach for constant fighting. In the face of any kind of determined defence he disengaged. Constant attacks, no matter how trifling the damage, discouraged him and were sure to bring a talk of peace. With good scouting to prevent surprise and ambush, even small bodies like Bridger's trappers could maintain themselves continuously in hostile Indian country. General Dodge says he solved his problem of reëstablishing the lines of communication by ordering his troops to make a bold front, and to keep their face continually, whether advancing or retreating, to the face of the enemy.

# CHAPTER XVI

### ARAPAHO IN THE COPSE

JIM BRIDGER was nearly sixty years of age when he first took service as an army scout in these Indian troubles. As a mountain man they had spoken of him affectionately as "Old" Gabe; it was "Old" Jim at the trading post, but now it was really old Jim Bridger. The bear-cat vigor of his mountain days was gone, and the strenuous life he had lived had taken toll of him in other ways. A quarter century of wading in ice-cold streams after beaver had left him a touch of rheumatism; the snow water he had lived on for years had brought on a goitre; he had a double rupture so that army officers

who knew him wondered that he could sit a
horse; his old wounds were giving him trouble;
and his eyesight was somewhat dimmed though
still pretty good. A soldier who was with him
in some Indian scraps during these scouting days
says that Jim Bridger cursed them roundly when
they had a chance for a shot and missed, saying
that he had never missed a shot at an Indian
when he was their age. Incidentally rifles were
now loaded at the breech, and were rapidly to
give way to repeating rifles. Six-shooters were
in common use.

One of Bridger's first assignments was to scout
for a detachment sent into the South Park of the
Colorado. Capt. J. Lee Humfreville, who was
in command, tells of an incident that shows there
was a considerable spryness in old Bridger yet.
The column, attacked by a large number of
mounted Indians, took up a good defensive position. Some of the advanced scouts of the hostiles slipped off their horses, and began to stalk
the position. They crawled into the brush and
began working their way towards the camp.
Bridger's trappers knew this kind of fighting
but soldiers were of little use in such encounters.
There were, however, some friendly Indians
with the column, and Bridger wanted them to
go in and drive the hostiles out. They declined

and Bridger after giving the chief a talking to in the sign language, slipped into the grass taking only his revolver. Snaking his way towards the advancing scouts, he got the first of them with a shot from his revolver and scalped him, putting an end to the advance by that means. Later he fired the brush with the help of the friendly Indians.

The main party of the Indians now coming up, the mounted men attempted to advance on the column. The first to get within range was brought down—a shot from Bridger's rifle. Discouraged the Indians hung around, and Bridger would not allow Humfreville to move his men until he had made sure that the hostiles had retired.

No wonder Capt. Humfreville could only speak of Bridger in superlatives. He refers to Bridger as the most efficient guide, mountaineer, plainsman, trapper, and Indian fighter that ever flourished in the far west; as a man who did not know what fear was; a marvelous trailer, "unquestionably the most expert in this line that ever lived." He also says that many of the famous mountain men and scouts of the western country were trained by Bridger; that it was Bridger who brought Kit Carson to the notice of General Fremont, and adds, "I have seen Carson take his orders and instructions from Bridger as a soldier does from his commanding officer."

Some of the men to whom Humfreville refers as being trained by Bridger as scouts are Jim Baker, Jim Beckwourth, Joe Meek, who had probably learned a great deal from Bridger while serving in his trapper commands. Carson was a trapper with Bridger and subject to the discipline of the brigades. Humfreville's statement would be interesting if we knew when he had seen the two great scouts together. The facts about Carson's employment by Fremont are these: They met on a Missouri steamboat, when the latter had set out to make his survey of the South Pass road. To continue in Kit's own words: "I spoke to Col. Fremont, informed him that I had been some time in the mountains and thought I could guide him to any point he would want to go. He replied that he would make inquiries regarding my capabilities of performing that which I promised. He done so. I presume he received reports favorable of me, for he told me I would be employed." Bridger and Fitzpatrick were the natural sources to which Fremont would direct his inquiries, and it is probable that Bridger spoke enthusiastically for Kit.

Bridger's services as an army scout, which

began in 1863 were continued with a few inter-
ruptions, for six years. The army paid him
sometimes as much as twenty-five dollars a day,
a general's salary, supplying him with his arms,
horse, equipment, food and other expenses. He
wintered that year in Fort Laramie and much
of the following year he spent in that neighborhood. It was the period of the Indian depredations that we have spoken of in the preceding
chapter, and there was a great deal of work close
at hand.

This was the beginning of the Sioux era that
was for several years to mark them as the most
formidable Indian tribe we had to deal with on
the plains. Their name comes to us from the
corruption of an Indian word that means "Enemy." Their own designation of their tribe is
"Dacotah" meaning "Friendly." In several
branches they were spread from the great lakes
to the mountains. Now they were to cut such a
formidable figure that a half a dozen or more
of their chiefs were to become almost household
words to the American public—Spotted Tail,
Red Cloud, Crazy Horse, Sitting Bull, Kicking
Bear, Rain-in-the-Face, American Horse, Even-
his-Horse-is-Feared.

Bridger had first seen them, when as friendly
allies they had fought with Ashley's trappers

against the 'Rees. They had played almost no
part in his life in the mountains, although he
had met them on a number of occasions while
crossing the plains.

From those early days there comes to us a
story of a hand-to-hand encounter that was typical of hundreds told about Bridger during his
lifetime. With an advance party of five men he
was pushing ahead of the fur train when they
were beset by an overwhelming force of Sioux.
Hobbling their horses, and building a barricade
with their packs, the party met the Sioux with
a galling fire. The fight grew so hot, however,
that every one of the white men was wounded,
and when night brought them a respite, they felt
that their only chance of surviving the morrow
was for some one to reach the main party with
a call for help.

Bridger volunteered for the task, although
wounded. Slipping out on foot, and stealing
like a ghost through the shadows, he was almost
through the Indian cordon and an Indian sleep-
ing near by, when the Sioux's horse, scenting the
white man, began to neigh. Indian horses and
mules grew just as alarmed over the approach
of white men as white men's horses did over the
approach of Indians. The Indian was on his
feet in the instant of the alarm. To fire a shot

would call every Indian within miles. There was only one thing for Bridger to do, and he did it immediately. He closed with the Sioux, killed him after a short struggle, jumped the Indian's horse and raced for the main body of the trappers.

The Sioux gradually pushed their influence west and north into the mountains. In 1841 the presence of one of their parties in the mountains was so plainly menacing, that Bridger sent Jim Baker to warn a party of trappers under Fraeb to be on their guard. Fraeb and a few others were killed in a determined attack lasting several days.

Two years later, the year Bridger built his fort, the Sioux and the Cheyennes left their visiting card on him, raiding his valley of the Green River and killing a number of Snake Indians. A year or so later Bridger, taking a bunch of tenderfeet on a trapping excursion far into northern Montana, came down to the junction of the Missouri and Yellowstone, and there had another run-in with the Sioux. The Indians ran off with a few of the trappers' horses. Bridger trailed them. The Indians took up a nice position on a hill, and invited him to come up and fight. This was nothing new, and

Bridger's old command of trappers knew the way to answer it. But, oh! for the days of the Iroquois hunter; Bridger now called to his trappers to come up with him, but none of them was game to take the odds. In disgust he disbanded the whole party and returned to his fort alone.

Though his contacts with the Sioux in the mountains had been comparatively few, these Indians knew him well by reputation. While guiding Capt. Stansbury in the survey of the Overland route a number of the Sioux visited their encampment. Stansbury makes the following note of the scene that ensued: "Our esteemed friend and experienced mountaineer, Major Bridger, who was personally known to many of our visitors, and to all of them by the repute of his numerous exploits, was sitting among us. Although intimately acquainted with the language of the Crows, Blackfeet, and most of the tribes * west and northwest of the Rocky Mountain chain, he was unable to speak to either the Sioux or the Cheyennes in their own tongue, or with any tribe they could understand.

"Notwithstanding this he held the whole circle for more than an hour perfectly enchained

* He could also speak fluently the Snake, Bannock, Flathead, Nez Perce, Pend d'Oreille, and Ute tongues. He may have learned some of the plains languages after the incident narrated above.

and evidently most deeply interested in the conversation and narrative, the whole of which was
carried on without the utterance of a single word.
The simultaneous exclamations of surprise or
interest, and the occasional bursts of hearty
laughter, showed that the whole party perfectly
understood not only the theme but the minutiæ
of the pantomime exhibited before them.    I
looked on with the closest attention, but the signs
to me were for the most part altogether unintel-
ligible.    Upon after inquiry I found that this
language of signs is universally understood by
all the tribes."

In the dozen years that had elapsed since the
Stansbury experience, Bridger had been a great
deal on the plains, so that when he took service
with the army as a scout he was known to them
not only for what he had been, but for what they
knew he could do.    He was no longer The
Blanket Chief, as the mountain Indians spoke
of him.    His goitre marked him out now.    The
Sioux called him "Big Throat."

The Sioux, like all the fighting plains tribes,
were superb horsemen, and their tactics in flat
country without cover is indelibly stamped on
our mind through the story of numerous conflicts.    They rode, sometimes with no more than
a rope hitched around the jaw of their horses,

keeping them under perfect control even at a
break-neck pace. Turning, whirling, circling,
advancing and retreating they made the most difficult target for our rifle-men. On one or two
occasions, fighting even a corralled wagon train
of soldiers shooting from behind cover, they have
been known to deliver so effective a fire that
every man was killed, though such a result is
somewhat freakish. They picked up their
wounded whenever it was possible if they disengaged in battle, two men riding at the wounded
man side by side, reaching down and picking
him up as they swept past.

This is General Dodge's estimate of the men
he was called on to combat: "The Indians of the
plains are the best skirmishers in the world. In
the rapidity of movements, in perfect horsemanship, sudden whirling, protecting the body by
clinging to the side of the horse, and rapid movements in open and difficult ground, no trained
cavalry in the world could equal them. On foot
their ability to hide behind any obstruction, any
ravine, along creeks and in creek and river banks,
and in fighting in the open plains or level
ground, the faculty to disappear is beyond one's
belief except he has experienced it. In skulking
and sharpshooting they are adepts.

"In a fight, the Indians will select the positions and pick out quickly any vantage ground, and sometimes as high as two hundred will concentrate at such a point where we could not concentrate twenty men without exposing them, and from this vantage ground they will pour a deadly fire on the troops and we cannot see an Indian, only puffs of smoke. By such tactics as this they harass and defeat our troops."

The Indians did their most deadly work by taking the troops off guard. Their superior plains lore and woodcraft allowed them to keep a body of troops constantly under their eye until an opportunity came to catch the soldiers at a disadvantage. On the warpath their scouts gave them a full knowledge of all troops in the vicinity. The troops in their stockades or on the march, on the other hand, had little knowledge regarding the movement of Indians, and chasing a few raiders had again and again, during 1863 and 1864, led to a trap, the fleeing Indians proving nothing but decoys. Surprise and ambush were the essentials of their tactics as with the forest and mountain redmen.

To counteract this disadvantage the government employed its civilian and Indian scouts, and their best work as often as not is read in their preventing the columns they guided falling into ambuscades, losing their horses, and getting

into a score of difficulties that seemed to beset
nearly every column setting out into the Indian
country.

In this period the chief job of the garrisons
in Indian country was to prevent further raids.
Bridger had been for many years now a celebrated figure, and while he was at Laramie a
great many officers sought him out and listened
to his incomparable yarns.  One of the officers—
Lt. Eugene F. Ware, who writes of Bridger,
"He knew everything an Indian knew.  He
could do anything that an Indian could do.  He
knew how Indians felt, and what to expect of
them," says that Bridger did little actual scouting during the two or three months Ware was at
that post.  Officers and guides setting out would
come to Bridger, who would tell them "where to
go and what they would find."

## CHAPTER XVII

### Scout Eyes and Officers' Glasses

FOLLOWING their raids on the plains during the winter of 1864-65, the hostile Sioux, Cheyennes and Arapahoes withdrew into the Powder River country, once the home of the Crows, but now regarded by the Sioux as their own hunting grounds. They were loaded with loot, and proposed to take their rest and recreation hunting the buffalo. The winter on the plains had been a bitter one with the thermometer sometimes showing twenty degrees below zero. General Dodge felt that this was a good time to carry the war into the Indians' own country, and he accordingly ordered an expedi-

tion to proceed into the Powder and Tongue
River country and attack every encampment of
Arapahoes, Sioux and Cheyennes they found.
Three columns were detailed to carry out the
design, General Patrick E. Connor being placed
in command of the entire expedition.

Bridger was chosen by General Dodge to be
the chief of scouts for the expedition. The general had known Bridger for a number of years
and he placed a very high estimate on the services Bridger could render such an undertaking.
He knew that when Jim Bridger was scouting
not a single horse or Indian could cross the trail
without the sign being discovered; that nothing
would escape his vision "the dropping of a stick
or breaking of a twig, the turning of the growing
grass," that they would each telegraph their message to this complete master of plains and woodcraft regarding who or what had done it, and
when. General Connor in turn attached Bridger
to his own staff, and detailed him to guide his
own column.

The plan of the campaign was for two columns, one under command of Col. N. Cole
marching from Columbus, Nebraska; the other
commanded by Col. Walker, setting out from
Fort Laramie, Wyo., to unite their forces west
of the Black Hills, march east to the Powder

River and follow it upstream, while the column under General Connor, setting out a little later, also from Laramie, would march north to the headwaters of the Powder and follow it downstream until they met.

Bridger had first traversed this country more than forty years ago with Provot during the fall trapping expedition that led to the discovery of South Pass, and he knew it like a book. He led the General's column, consisting of about seven hundred and fifty troopers and infantrymen, with seventy-five Pawnee Indians under Capt. Frank North and about the same number of Winnebago and Omaha Indians, across the Platte and to the headwaters of the Powder. There the column halted for some time while they built a fort that was afterwards known as Fort Reno. Here General Connor left a garrison, and with the balance of his men continued down the river.

The march down the Powder River gives us one or two "flashes" of how Jim Bridger, the scout, worked. He slept in a little tent of his own. He was up each morning before sunrise and cooked a frugal meal, consisting usually of coffee and jerked meat. He would then call on General Connor and having received his instructions would ride off and disappear until the

WILD PURSUIT

night's camp was made, when he would ride in, report to the General, then go into his tent, again cook his own meal, and as soon as it was dark wrap his blanket around himself and go to sleep. He was close-mouthed and would hardly talk to any one except the commander and officers in charge while on such duty, although he was ready enough to swap a yarn at Fort Laramie or elsewhere when conditions were different.

On the march he rode the center of the scout line, with the Pawnees and other Indians taking the flanks. One of the officers who rode with him in advance occasionally says that Bridger once tried to explain to him how he could tell the different tribes of Indians by their tracks. The officer was too much of a tenderfoot to be able to grasp what Bridger was saying to him, alas! Was Bridger speaking of horse or moccasin tracks? All the plains Indians rode their horses unshod (the mountain Indians shod them with buffalo hide); and the moccasin itself leaves so faint an imprint that it is hard to tell it, let alone distinguish one tribe footprint from another. Later on in this campaign he did actually inform the command of the presence of a large body of Indians, giving their numbers, the number of their horses and the animals they had stolen—complete and accurate information regarding the whole force of hostiles without having seen a single one of them, which was verified in the subsequent engagement.

The march of the Connor column, small though it was in numbers, was a triumphal journey. They swept everything they met before them. A party of twenty-four Cheyennes whose trail was encountered, were followed by the Pawnee scouts and killed to a man, without suffering any casualties other than four horses which were lost.

The most dramatic fight in this campaign is prefaced by an amusing anecdote concerning a report Bridger made early one morning of a large Indian encampment in the distance. Riding in advance of the column, behind the haze that covered the hills and valleys, he spied the smoke of the Indians' early morning camp fires. An officer accompanying the advance patrols looked through his glasses and was sure that what he saw was nothing more than the haze. Bridger was insistent and they waited for General Connor. He, too, looked hard and long in the direction indicated and gave as his opinion that it was nothing but a haze.

Bridger was highly wroth, and walked away muttering something about "these damn paper-collar soldiers telling him there was no columns of smoke." He was a person of importance, and even generals did not like to treat him with what seemed like discourtesy. More to satisfy the old man than to assure himself of the report, General Connor ordered a small detachment of North's Pawnees to reconnoiter the position that Bridger had marked. It was forty or fifty miles away. Of course, Bridger's dimmed eyesight was not superior to the vision of the officers looking through army field glasses. A hundred little indications from the training of a lifetime told him things, which it was impossible to explain to men who had no conception of these differences.

Presently, word came from North's Pawnees that the smoke Bridger had seen came from a large encampment of Arapahoes. Word was sent to the scouts to hold it under observation. Four hundred men, with General Connor at their head, and guided by Bridger, made a forced march during the night. Without the Indians being in any way alarmed, the column was brought within less than a mile of the camp, and wheeled into line. A bugle was sounded, a volley fired, and the troops charged. The Indians were in superior force, but the whole encampment was caught flat-footed, and a large number of them were killed. The village was destroyed. Some women and children, and nearly all the Indian horses were captured, the former being released after a few days. A number of Indians, bolting like rabbits at the first alarm, managed to escape. The Pawnees took charge of the horse herd, nearly a thousand horses and mules, and succeeded in driving most of them back. A soldier who took part in the charge says of Bridger that during the fighting he turned up constantly at the right place at the right time. Good scouting had demonstrated that the Indian could be caught by white men through the very tactics that had proved him such a terror as a raider.

If that engagement conclusively proved the value of good scouting, the whole expedition was soon to have a vivid, if unhappy, demonstration of the vital place the good guide and scout had in making for the success or failure of such enterprises. General Connor's column had not only been marching and fighting with practically no casualties, but the comfort and security of the column was such that the officers behaved as if they were on a picnic, getting a great deal of sport in hunting.

Failing to connect with the columns under the command of Colonels Cole and Walker, General Connor ordered Capt. Frank North to take some of his Pawnee scouts and try to locate them. The joint Cole-Walker column formed a party twice as large as the Connor column. When North succeeded in finding them the whole command was unhorsed and on the point of starvation. They had only engaged the Indian when forced to do so; had lost a great number of their horses; were forced to shoot the rest at the picket lines and to burn all their equipment and supplies for fear they would fall into the hands of the hostiles. The men were in rags and so hungry that soldiers offered their Pawnee rescuers five dollars for a piece of hardtack, which the Indians refused to take, giving the soldiers everything they had. North led the Cole-Walker column to Fort Reno, where Connor joined them shortly after, the whole scheme of giving the raiding Indians a lesson in their own country being largely frustrated.

The Cole-Walker party had no adequate guides. They wandered about the country, often not sure where they were. One weather-wise scout like Jim Bridger would have prevented their being caught in storms, found them protecting ground where their horses could be pastured, and prevented others from being run off. It was only a miracle that had saved the whole worn and dispirited party from being massacred by the Sioux in their vicinity. But the Powder River expedition had its value. It showed the Indian that raiding was something he would have to answer for in war carried into his own villages.

General Connor was recalled from the Indian country, and Bridger went back to his Kansas City farm to spend the winter with his family, one of the few he was to spend with them in these active years. It is probable that young Felix was also home, having been mustered out from service at the conclusion of the Civil War, and that a few yarns were swapped between them of fighting in the South and of forays in the Indian country.

# CHAPTER XVIII

## SIGN ON THE BUFFALO SKULL

THE development of the white civilian scouts with the army was an accident. Bridger had a great deal to do with making them almost indispensable in Indian campaigns, and with establishing them as the romantic figure they became to the American public. The first employment of such men as Bridger was as guides. They knew the country, its trails, crossings and passes, and they were chosen to show the way, and give advice with regard to camping places, weather signs, good pasturage and other information that would be of value to a commander in making his plans for the march. Experience with these trapper-scouts, however, soon brought out the fact that they were even more valuable in military reconnaissance.

The trapper-scouts were a remarkable group. They had built up the principles they applied to scouting through long years of experience, when as trappers they had lived constantly in Indian country, heavily outnumbered by almost every party they ran up against. Their lore included not only the tactics Indians employed in battle, and the most intimate understanding of how Indians thought, felt and acted in all circumstances, but added much in the way of forest, plains and mountain lore all their own, with a touch of military tactics that made them competent advisers to an army command. Bridger's small command of trappers that bearded the Blackfeet in their den, had a discipline as strict as any applied to a body of soldiers, although there was nothing in the way of drills, standing to attention, loud commands and all that. The trappers were in a sense the most complete and efficient scouts that our frontiers have known, but more than this, the principles they developed were so sound that they could be applied to country that was totally unknown, and to enemies that differed radically in their tactics from

the cunning Indian. Major Frederick R. Burn-
ham, who as a youngster was trained by some
old scouts of this trapper school, found that he
could apply those principles in scouting against
the Zulu and the Boer, with results almost daz-
zling in their effectiveness.

With the passing of Bridger, although the
plains were to see a great many scouts who became famous, they were largely lacking in the
experience and knowledge the trapper-scouts
possessed. The army came more and more to
depend on friendly Indian scouts with civilians,
and sometimes qualified army men, designated
as their chiefs. Humfreville says frankly that
a scout like Jim Bridger would never have allowed Custer's command to be caught and massacred on the Little Big Horn. Custer's scouts
gave him no idea of the force to which he was
opposed, and he divided his troops in the face
of greater numbers, falling prey to a simple
straight-on charge of an overwhelming number
of Indians, one of the few occasions on which
the Indians won a complete victory without
their favorite tactics of ambush or surprise.

Bridger who had found time between his scout
engagements at Laramie and the Powder River
expedition in 1864 to convoy a train of gold
seekers to Montana, and who had predicted that

trouble would ensue from the emigrants passing through Sioux country on the Bozeman trail, found that prophecy more than fulfilled in the troubles that immediately developed. Now his vacation with his family was cut short and he was called on (January 1866) to pilot Col. Henry B. Carrington, who was ordered to take a small expedition on the Bozeman trail, to set up and garrison a couple of forts for the protection of the emigrants, and keep the trail open.

The humorous part of this expedition is that it was sent by the government to permanently occupy a part of the country with seven hundred and fifty men, the year following the Powder River expedition when nearly three times that number had run into serious difficulties. Col. Carrington (later General) had no experience of the Indian country or of Indian fighting. Two-thirds of his men were raw recruits. They were armed with old muzzle-loading rifles, although a few had breech-loaders. The ammunition they were supplied with was so inadequate that none could be spared for the recruits to practice shooting. This attempt to make a road through their country had by now stung the Sioux to fighting frenzy. It looked like a perfect preliminary setting for a "heap big" Indian scalp dance that was to follow.

But Carrington had Jim Bridger. From the first General Carrington looked on Bridger not only as scout and guide, but his confidential adviser. As they went through Laramie a peace conference was in session, through which the government hoped to buy a cessation of hostilities on the Bozeman trail. But it did not deceive anybody who was conversant with the Indian situation, least of all Bridger who sat at the sessions listening to the speeches. None of the Sioux leaders who were responsible for the hostilities were present, and there was as much chance of binding them to a treaty they did not make as to keep a white man from going after gold because it was dangerous.

To add to Carrington's troubles, and the natural concern he felt over the whole enterprise, the War Department was having a fit of economy. General Philip St. George Cooke, in command of the department, looked over Carrington's payroll and saw an item which he felt could be eliminated and would reduce expenses. He directed Carrington to discharge his chief guide, James Bridger! Carrington, however, had already learned Bridger's value. He was setting out on the march from Laramie immediately, and could avoid questions. He wrote across General Cooke's order: "Impossible of Execution," and continued Bridger on his payroll.

The route Carrington followed was much the same as that taken the year previous by Connor's column. Carrington stopped at Fort Reno, built last year by General Connor, put it in shape, garrisoned it, and proceeded down the Powder River with the balance of his men.

The commander's wife, another lady and one or two children accompanied the column. They went through to the site of the first new fort they were to put up, almost without incident, except for seeing the stock from an emigrant train run off at Fort Reno. These people believed that the stories of Indian depredations were grossly exaggerated, and the vigilance that had been urged on them unnecessary. The captain of the train had scarcely finished saying so when a sudden tumult showed their horses pasturing near the fort were being first stampeded and then lashed at a gallop into the hills.

From this period also comes down to us one "flash" of the remarkable quality Bridger put into his scouting. General Carrington wanted some supplies from Fort Reno. He ordered a small detachment under Capt. Burrows to go back for them, assigning Bridger to convoy the party. One day Bridger, scouting ahead of the column, galloped back and urged Burrows to push his men as hard as he could, for some distance away, he said, at Crazy Woman's fork, the Indians were besieging a wagon train.  As Crazy Woman was too far away for Bridger to have seen it, and not being anxious to push his command beyond the camping place they had planned for the night, Burrows was not willing to set out on a wild goose chase.  How did Bridger know what was taking place in some place he had not seen?  The reason Bridger gave him seemed to Burrows as crazy as the name of the place to which the scout was urging him to ride.  He could understand that Bridger might be able to tell the presence of Indians by the action of a bird, a buffalo or an antelope, or that he could tell who and what had passed from signs on the ground, but setting time and place of Indians making an attack at a distant point was quite another thing.  He was not inclined to move.  But Bridger was so insistent, and he was held in so great respect, that Burrows felt he could not disregard the scout's appeal.

As soon as Burrows consented to follow him, Bridger sent his horse into a lope ahead of the column.  Late that evening the train, engaged in a desperate defence with a band of Indians, constantly increasing in number, saw a cloud of dust appear on the horizon, and the Indians pull out suddenly and disappear in all directions. The emigrants were still in corral when a lone horseman came riding towards it. They were standing by their rifles, suspicious of further attack.

"Who are you?" they shouted.

"I am Jim Bridger," he answered.

What was the "sign" Capt. Burrows had thought so fantastic? Bridger had told him that the buffalo skulls on the plains were carrying a message from the Sioux saying that they were making an attack on a wagon train at Crazy Woman, and that all Indians were invited to come and take part in it.

It's too bad that we have lost the details of how the buffalo skulls were made to spell out that message. Bridger's trappers frequently wrote messages to various parties on buffalo skulls and placed them on the trail the others would cross, just as they invented the bent twig, stone and many other trail indicators we use to-day. The Indians sometimes used crude pictures to convey a message. Nearly all the tribes had a code by which a stone or a skull turned in a certain way would indicate time of the day or night. Place, too, might be shown by the way the object was placed. Since pictures would give them away to every white man that passed, undoubtedly in this case the method used must have been the latter.  It is easy enough to do this as a prearranged signal, that is, if anybody wants to meet you secretly, to turn a stone so that it will point the hour and perhaps to a place. Bridger's difficulty in convincing Burrows of the authenticity of the sign he read suggests that he puzzled out the message by a series of deductions too complicated to convince the captain of their reasonableness.

Mrs. Carrington, who wrote a book about her experiences on this expedition, has a number of interesting things to say regarding Jim Bridger: "There was one faithful, honest and simple minded white man of the best, the colonel's confidential guide at all times, who seemed instinctively to know the invisible as well as the visible operations of the Indian, good old Jim Bridger. His devotion to the ladies and children, and his willingness to cheer them up as best he could, were as prized as were his quaint tales of his long experience."  "His genial manners and simplicity of bearing commanded respect as well as attachment and confidence of all who knew him well."  When it looked as if there was nothing stirring in the world around them, she says, Bridger could see Indian scouts on every hill and behind every bush; he was most alert when there seemed the least activity on the part of Indians.

General Carrington's troubles began when he started to build Fort Phil Kearney.

# CHAPTER XIX

## Meet Shakespeare, Mr. Bridger

MRS. CARRINGTON was one of a number of people who found a great deal of entertainment in reading to Jim Bridger. It was a very natural curiosity and interest that led them to seek his opinions on the books read to him, for the old frontiersman, so shrewd and wise in his own world, could neither read nor write, and in the world of books he was a tenderfoot on a strange trail.

Among Bridger's trappers of the old mountain days had been many well-educated men, familiar with the classics in English, Latin, Greek and other languages. Some of them prob-

ably carried well-thumbed volumes, which must
have been read during the long evenings of the
winter encampments. No hint comes down to
us from those days of Bridger being drawn into
such a circle. From his contacts during his
trail-breaking and scouting days, however, there
is a record of a number of instances in which
books and Jim Bridger were introduced to each
other.

Sir George Gore in the grand hunting trip he
made spent evening after evening reading to
Bridger. We have only a "flash" of that long
experience, for it survives largely in a few para-
graphs written by an army officer, reporting a
conversation he had with Bridger about the
books Gore read to him. One of them was "The
Adventures of Baron Munchausen," whom
Bridger referred to as "the durned liar." Gore
also read to Bridger Sir Walter Scott's description of the battle of Waterloo. At the conclusion of this reading the Baronet turned to
Bridger and asked him if he did not think that
was the bloodiest battle ever fought. Bridger
was impressed, but not overcome. He remarked:
"Wall, now, Mr. Gore, that thar must 'a' bin a
considdible of a skrimmage, dogon my skin ef it
mustn't"; and added, "them thar Britishers must
'a' fit better thar than they did down to Horleans

whar Old Hickory gin un the forkedest sort o' chain-lightnin' that perhaps you ever did see in all yer born days!" Sir George doubted that the battle of New Orleans was the fight Bridger thought it was, and Bridger assured him that "you can just go yer pile on it, Mr. Gore, you can, as sure as yer born." Shakespeare, Bridger then felt, was a little too "high falutin' for him." Capt. (later General) R. B. Marcy, the man who made the epic winter journey across the Uinta mountains during the Mormon war, who is responsible for these anecdotes, is the only one who has tried to reproduce Bridger's dialect, and it does not seem very convincing.

Mrs. Carrington says Bridger listened to the reading of Shakespeare "with unfeigned pleasure." Between the Gore and Carrington readings, he had quite a course in Shakespeare, as you will see. Mrs. Carrington read to him from the Bible, too, and mentions his special interest in the Samson story. This was a good mountain man's yarn, but what arrested Bridger's attention was that part of it which tells of Samson's actions following the betrayal by his Philistine wife of the answer to a riddle he had propounded to thirty young Philistines and on which he had made a sizable wager. Samson came back, after taking it out on the young Philistines, not in wrath but in the most forgiving spirit, to his wife, to find only that her father had given her in marriage to one of Samson's friends.

Samson proceeded thereupon to revenge himself on the Philistines. He caught three hundred foxes, tied them tail to tail, put a firebrand at each juncture and turned them loose. The coupled foxes immediately ran wild, setting fire not only to the corn that was already shocked, but to wheat that was standing, to the vineyards, and olive groves.

Here was a trick that no pesky Blackfoot or raiding Sioux had ever dreamed on! Jim Bridger knew every Indian trick along these lines; he knew about catching foxes and firing green stuff too, and reluctantly decided that after all here was no trick that would come in handy in Indian fighting.

Capt. J. Lee Humfreville's contribution to Bridger-and-the-books stories is a little different. The captain took to the books not to find out how Bridger felt about this or that, but purely in self-defence. Returning with Bridger to Fort Laramie after the South Park expedition in 1863, they spent the winter there together. Humfreville found the old scout's routine was so unorthodox that he was kept up night after night. Bridger wrapped his blanket around

himself and went to sleep when he was sleepy;
he cooked a meal and ate it when he was hungry.
Since he went to bed very early at night that
was bad enough, but even worse was the fact
that if Bridger woke up in the middle of the
night and the urge to sleep was not there, he
would proceed to entertain himself, using a tin
pail or anything else handy for a tom-tom, and
crooning away at Indian chants of which he had
a great store. Humfreville decided that drastic
steps must be taken to keep Bridger awake late
enough at night so that he would sleep through
until the morning. He hit upon the idea of
reading to Bridger until it was time to go to
bed.

"Hiawatha" was pressed into service. Bridger
listened to Longfellow's lines, occasionally a
little restlessly, but night after night until he had
enough of it. Then he would rise, pretending
to be wrathful, and exclaim: "It's a lie. No
Indian like that ever lived."

A few days later, however, he asked Humfreville what was the best book in the world, and
the captain answered "Shakespeare." Among
the wagon trains Bridger found an emigrant who
had a copy of the plays and was willing to trade
it, Bridger giving him a yoke of oxen worth a
hundred and twenty-five dollars. He hired an

emigrant boy who could read well, at forty dollars a month, to read it to him, and evening after evening, with Humfreville in attendance, he gave himself a course in Shakespeare. When occasionally he lost the thread of the story he would have the boy go back and read a page or two. At Richard III he declared he did not want to read about a man who had been mean enough to kill his mother (it is not clear how Bridger got this from the play), flung the books into the fire, and was done with them.

This was interesting and amusing; the natural reaction of a simple-minded, ruggedly honest, unlettered frontiersman, but we are not so sure Bridger was not having some fun all his own. Lt. Ware who met Bridger the following summer tells this anecdote—or another—as a great joke on Bridger. The details he gives are very different. He says Bridger saw some soldier actor put on a Shakespearean play and was so impressed that he hired a soldier to read to him, quitting again at Richard III. Mrs. Carrington's story told about Bridger during her husband's campaign two years later, strongly suggests that he did have during that time another course in Shakespeare, and her version of the Richard III story may be quite a different incident to the one told by Humfreville. She says that when Bridger came to the story of the Princes in the Tower he asked that it be read again to make sure that they had been foully done to death.   He quit then, remarking that "Shakespeare must have had a bad heart and been as devilish as a Sioux to have written such scoundrelism as that."

Another reason which makes us feel that Bridger may have been doing a little sly laughing is this: Humfreville tells us that after Bridger's first earnest course in Shakespeare so good was his memory and grip of the lines read to him that he could reel off quotation after quotation from the plays; and that frequently he would interpolate phrases of his own in the quotations so adroitly that his listeners found it impossible to tell which was Bridger and which Shakespeare!

# CHAPTER XX

## SIGNALS

THE Sioux made it plain when General Carrington started to build Fort Phil Kearney that they were determined to throw him out of their country, and to bar the emigrant road to Montana. What Carrington did in five months—July to December, handicapped as he was, is remarkable. In spite of constant raids that resulted in from one to three fights a day, he completed Fort Phil Kearney, cutting and hauling his timber from some woods about seven miles away; he then built another fort—Fort C. F. Smith—about a hundred miles further to the northwest; and had Bridger, as we have noted elsewhere, make a survey of the route, measuring the distance in miles, and straightening it out in a few places.

The tenderfeet of Carrington's command were not equal to combating the cunning of the Indian in stealing horses, but so well were they protected that they held their own excellently in the fighting, giving as good as they got. The casualties on either side, however, were not great. For this result, Bridger, growing increasingly old and feeble, as Carrington's confidential adviser, deserves more than a little credit. The most vulnerable part of the command was, of course, the woods train, but this was a method of fighting Bridger had a great deal of experience in. The woods-road, running through open ground, provided a good open field for rifle fire. The wagons were organized to move two abreast, and taught in Indian attack to form a circle, horses in the center, wagons standing wheel to wheel. A howitzer at the fort, firing a shell with about eighty bullets, was used to scatter any attempt of the Sioux to concentrate in numbers for an attack; a small party could be handled easily from the corralled wagons. A sortie from the fort would drive the Indians off if they were too persistent and force them over the ridge. As to the fort itself no attack was made on it, though a few Indians would occasionally ride within gunshot out of bravado, making the usual difficult target with their trick riding.

Bridger not only saw Indian scouts on "every hill and behind every bush," but he was constantly reading their signals, and knew just what their attacks meant—raids by a few jaunty braves, a cunning decoy, or simple gasconading. The heliograph invented by a British officer in India was first used by the American army during the Apache campaign of 1885. General Nelson A. Miles in his Recollections tells of how impressed Geronimo was by that beam of light flashing from hilltop stations. Yet here was Bridger some twenty years earlier reading the messages of Indians signaling with mirrors. Those flashes, coming in the morning and evening when the sun slashed down into the valleys, seemed to the soldiers only an accidental reflection from a stone or some other bright object. What Bridger said of the use of mirrors by Indians in signaling was subsequently borne out by army officers who made a study of Indian tactics in war.

As the Indian had no standard alphabetical code, such as we have in the Morse and semaphore, he used, apart from certain standard

signs, a great many arbitrary signals agreed on
for a special purpose, and decoding them was
often a matter of clever deduction. In "Indian
lore" to-day all that survives are a few Indian
signals made with smoke broken into puffs by
the use of a blanket over a fire, the smoke being
given a certain shape by the way in which the
blanket is jerked over and off the fire. The
plains and mountain Indians constantly used the
smoke or fire signal. One fire, made some distance from water, so that it would not be confused with a camp fire, would tell the whole
country "strangers are passing through," so that
even in peace-time the approach of a white party
would be heralded far in advance of their
coming.

Such a scout as Bridger was had a lore of Indian signs that would fill a book. The Indians
used not only the mirror and the smoke—the
Apaches made the latter famous—but the
blanket, the flint and steel, the actions of the
running scout if on foot, the maneuvers of his
horse if mounted, to tell a story to those behind,
who watched him carefully. An Indian scout
reconnoitering an encampment at night, would
turn his back on it, draw his blanket over him
to conceal the light, and strike sparks with his
flint and steel to send a message of what he had

learned. A series of messages could be sent by the manner in which the blanket was held or waved (there is a record of a Blackfoot chief signaling "no battle" to Bridger in this way during the mountain days). If an Indian on foot was seen chasing himself round and round in a circle as if he had suddenly gone mad, ten to one he was signaling some message of his discovery of an enemy of their disposition. A government troop chasing an Indian band would suddenly see, as they often did in those strenuous days, the fleeing horsemen break suddenly into two parties, ride out to the left and right, swing together again and cross each other—that or a dozen other crazy-looking movements. It was a good time to look out for a squall, for something would happen rapidly. They had a regular sign language made by the movements of a ridden horse. The white man at a distance could not even distinguish the movements that were clicking off a sure message to other Indians. Jim Bridger's eyes and the knowledge he carried in his head, were worth as much as the reinforcement of a thousand men to Carrington.

Another little testimony of Bridger's alertness as a scout comes down to us in the attention he paid the wolves. One of the favorite methods Indian scouts used in the mountains to make an approach in the open was to deck themselves out in the head and skin of an antelope. For night reconnaissance the wolf was much better, and plains and mountain Indians used it frequently, for the wolf naturally gravitates towards an encampment and noses around it. Kit Carson was once taken in by such a trick, when Indians succeeded in running off his horses. He was suspicious and approached close to the disguised Indian scout, who turned around with a wolf-snarl and then snapped its teeth at Kit's dog. The rattle, concealed in his hand, which the Indian used to make the sound of a wolf gritting its teeth, deceived Carson, so natural did it seem. For Bridger, wise on the trail in these days when he was the eyes of Carrington's command, the very numbers in which wolves appeared was a sure indication whether they were real wolves or lurking Indians. He would listen to the howl and pick them out. When he was doubtful he listened to the echo, finding that the how-oooo thrown back from the hills was an almost sure way of telling the difference between the real and the fake wolf.

Among the reënforcements sent to Carrington was a Brevet Lt. Col. William J. Fetterman, who had served in the Civil War and had come into the Indian country fully convinced that after battles in the south fighting Indians could only be a picnic. He was anxious to get a few scalps; "Red Cloud's" for preference among them. With a hundred men he would go through the Sioux country; with a company of regulars he would whip a thousand Sioux; with a thousand men he would lick every Indian tribe in existence. This attitude of the tenderfoot army officer was nothing new to Bridger. His comment regarding Fetterman's boast was to the point: "Your men who fought down south are crazy! They don't know anything about fighting Indians."

Carrington had felt all along that he had been inadequately provided with men and supplies for the task he had been given. He had used Bridger's vast experience as a substitute for his total unfamiliarity with the Indian country and its fighting, and he made a fine success of a most difficult job. Bridger had, during his survey of the Bozeman trail, come in touch with the Crows and learned from them that the Sioux were taking their failure to defeat Carrington to heart, and were planning a desperate attack. Carrington was not anxious, therefore, that Fetterman's hot-headedness should bring them to some disaster. In an attack on the woods train, the latter had been asked to relieve the train by a sortie. With forty men Fetterman had dashed after the Sioux, was following them over the ridge and was nearly surrounded, when Carrington coming up with a few men was able to get him out of the difficulty. Two friendly Cheyennes visiting the fort had been received by Bridger, shown the defences in a way that would make them feel it was impregnable, for he knew that they would convey this impression to the Sioux.

That made an attack in force on the fort itself unlikely. In the best of circumstances Indians disliked making open frontal attacks on fortifications, as by tactics and temperament they were unsuited to making a prolonged siege. Only by surprise could they hope to take the fort, and there was little chance of that with "Big Throat" behind the stockade. Their one chance was to lure Carrington's command or a large part of it into the open, and Bridger must have impressed this on Carrington, for we find the General fully sensitive to such a danger.

The first experience Col. Fetterman had with the Sioux had only encouraged his contempt of them. During a visit to the sawmill, he was ambushed by a number of their riflemen. Firing with a dead rest at point blank range they sent a volley at Fetterman and failed to touch him, so that he quite justly regarded them as atrocious marksmen. Another experience, however, might have taught him caution. Hoping to get a scalp or two, he took a mule and set it as bait, while he lay in wait for the Indians who would try to run it off. The Sioux horse-stealers left the bait alone, but shortly after Fetterman removed his mule, they raided the horse herd and ran off a number of them.

On December 21st an attack in some force was made by the Sioux on the woods train. The howitzer was fired, and Carrington ordered Major Powell to take a mixed force of infantry and cavalry amounting to ninety men and relieve the train. As senior officer Fetterman demanded this command. Carrington could not deny the request, but he gave Fetterman orders to drive off the Indians and on no account to pursue them over the ridge. To make sure Fetterman understood his orders, Carrington repeated them to him twice.

Fetterman did just what he was commanded not to do. He followed the Indians, who turned back to skirmish, just enough to keep both his infantry and cavalry advancing together. Some Indians appeared before the fort to divert attention from Fetterman. When these were driven off Fetterman's men had completely disappeared. Carrington sent all the men he could spare with orders to relieve Fetterman and order him back to the fort. There was some firing beyond the ridge and then an ominous silence. The relieving force when it got to the ridge could see a great number of Indians but not a single soldier.

Fetterman had been completely taken in by the oldest of Indian decoy tricks. They had used it times out of number on the garrisons on the plains. A few men mounted on swift horses would appear, and run before the chasing soldiers, leading them into a trap.

Not a man of Fetterman's command lived to tell the tale. The Indians withdrew after the slaughter and the relieving force advancing cautiously came upon the slain. About half the bodies they brought back that night; Carrington went out with about eighty men the next day and brought in the balance. Only a few of them had been killed by bullets or arrows; the large majority had fallen in hand to hand combat, so that it seems certain they were led into a very close trap. Fetterman and his second-in-command had shot themselves through the temple with their own revolvers.

The Fetterman disaster served to call attention to one of the most brilliant campaigns conducted in the Indian country. At the time of the disaster, with reënforcements, General Carrington had only six hundred and twenty-seven men. He had built two forts; had garrisoned them and Fort Reno as well; and kept communications open, running a regular weekly mail service. He was so poorly provided with ammunition that at one time the soldiers at Fort Smith were reduced to ten rounds per man. He had fought fifty-one skirmishes around Fort Phil Kearney alone. All this in the teeth of thousands of hostiles and in the very heart of the Sioux country. Well might General Carrington feel that the Fetterman disaster was simply a vindication of the value and integrity of Major Bridger, on whose experience he had relied to perform the miracle.

When news of the Fetterman massacre reached General P. St. George Cooke he promptly removed General Carrington from the command and hurried reënforcements. When General Sherman, Cooke's commanding officer, learned the facts, he as promptly removed General Cooke. There was a Presidential investigation, as a result of which the Bozeman trail was later abandoned.

When General Carrington marched from Fort Phil Kearney, Bridger was left behind, not to continue his scouting, but because he was "old and infirm." He was down with an attack of rheumatism, and his eyesight was steadily failing. There were one or two little jaunts left in him yet, however. He was on his feet in the summer and able to make the journey to Fort Laramie.

He had recovered sufficiently the following year to undertake one or two small scouting trips for the army, and was sent for by General P. H. Sheridan to Fort Hays, Kansas, and consulted with regard to a campaign in the southwest. It marks the end of Bridger's scouting days. He was too infirm to take the war-trail again.

# CHAPTER XXI

### TRAIL END

FOLLOWING his retirement from service as a government scout, Bridger lived nearly thirteen years with his family at Little Santa Fe farm in Jackson County, Missouri. The world grew steadily dimmer before those peerless eyes that used to "flash like an eagle." Soon he was left in complete darkness.

Nearly all the mountain men with whom he followed the beaver had by now passed on to the long trail. Old Broken Hand Fitzpatrick had been dead twenty years or more; the Sublettes, Campbell and the Rocky Mountain leaders were dead. Even the younger men, like Kit Carson,

had made their last journey. The army officers
with whom Bridger had campaigned were scattered far and wide, eager captains were now
stolid generals; generals passed into civilian life.

And so he slipped gently into days that were
strangely quiet for one who had lived so turbulent a life. Mrs. Bridger was dead. Virginia,
the daughter he had brought up on buffalo milk,
devoted her days to him. No longer were there
such dainties as the buffalo tongue or the beaver
tail to present to neighbors and friends. The
apple orchard had to do. He was proud of it,
and baskets of the fruit were sent as gifts to the
neighbors; he loved to talk with their children.
Out in the fields he could see the corn and the
wheat growing now only by the feel of his hands.
Occasionally the dogs raised a rabbit with a
brave cry, and old Jim hallo'ed after them ex-
citedly.

Virginia bought him a gentle horse, Ruff by
name, that he often rode, accompanied by Sultan,
a foxhound, as guardian. He could keep his
direction pretty well even though he could not
see, but sometimes the tiny woods on the farm
did what the whole wide west could not in other
days do. He would lose himself, and Sultan
racing home set up a great yapping that would
bring Virginia. During these days the house

at Westport, which he bought from Col. Boone's son, and a part of the farm, had to be sold to meet expenses.

His humor, and the gallant spirit from which it sprung was still alive. In years gone by some robbers once entered his lodge. Waking he had shouted, "What are you looking for?" "We are looking for your money," the desperadoes answered. "If you wait jest a minute," Bridger had replied, "I'll get up and help you."

When Father De Smet had asked him in the old mountain days how it was that his many wounds had not suppurated, he had answered, "In the mountains meat never spoils."

Now they asked him if there was anything he wished. The blue mountains and the vast plain had been home to him for forty-five years. Yes; he would like to be out there in the west. Why? He could by now see not even the shadow of his hand held in front of his eyes, but he answered as gamely, "In the country you can see so much further!"

No thought of fame, no desire to tell the world of his great adventures, seems to have ever moved him. Dozens of army officers who had known him as a scout had confidently expected that some famous man-of-letters would write the

story of Bridger's fabulous adventures, but
Bridger did not even keep in touch with these
men, choosing to slip out of life as humbly as
his career had begun.

He died July 17, 1881, and was buried on land
that had once been a part of his Little Santa Fe
farm. In a few years not a stone or a stick
marked the little grassy knoll of his last resting
place.

Some years later it occurred to General Grenville M. Dodge to inquire about Bridger, and
he was aghast to learn that the world that owed
so much to the great scout had so completely
forgotten the most distinguished frontiersman of
the far west. It hadn't really. Bridger had
merely slipped by, as in life he had slipped by
watchful Indian sentries. People were more
than willing to follow General Dodge's lead.
Mount Washington Cemetery in Kansas City
donated a prominent site. A monument, por-
traying Bridger's features taken from a photo-
graph, the only one in existence, was ordered
with an inscription written by General Dodge
himself.

General Dodge also wrote a biographical
sketch of James Bridger, which was read at the
public ceremony, and Jim Bridger's grand-

daughter, Marie Louise Lightle, unveiled the monument. The inscription reads:

1804—JAMES BRIDGER—1881

Celebrated as a hunter, trapper, fur-trader, and guide. Discovered Great Salt Lake, 1824; the South Pass, 1827. Visited Yellowstone Lake and geysers, 1830. Founded Fort Bridger, 1843. Opened Overland Route by Bridger's Pass to Great Salt Lake. Was guide for U. S. exploring expeditions, Albert Sidney Johnston's army in 1857, and G. M. Dodge in U. P. Surveys and Indian campaigns, 1865-66.

Printed in the United States
110743LV00004B/155/A